LETTERS

WRITTEN DURING THE

INDIAN MUTINY

LETTERS

WRITTEN DURING THE

INDIAN MUTINY

FRED ROBERTS

EDITOR

COUNTESS ROBERTS

GYAN

Published by

Gyan Publishing House
5, Ansari Road
Daryaganj, New Delhi-110002
Phone: 011-47034999, 9811692060
E-mail: books@gyanbooks.com

Distribution Network
gyanbooks.com
India, USA, Canada, UK, Australia

ISBN: 978-93-6920-159-4 (HB)

First Published, 1924

2nd Impression 2025

Printed at: Gyan Press, Delhi.

LETTERS WRITTEN DURING THE INDIAN MUTINY
Author: FRED ROBERTS, Editor: COUNTESS ROBERTS

LETTERS WRITTEN DURING THE INDIAN MUTINY

"Fred" Roberts (aet. 20)

From a pastel drawing by E. Grimston

LETTERS

WRITTEN DURING THE

INDIAN MUTINY

BY

FRED. ROBERTS

LIEUTENANT, BENGAL HORSE ARTILLERY
AND DEPUTY ASSISTANT QUARTERMASTER-GENERAL OF THE DELHI FIELD FORCE

AFTERWARDS

FIELD-MARSHAL EARL ROBERTS

V.C., K.G.

WITH A PREFACE BY HIS DAUGHTER

COUNTESS ROBERTS

MACMILLAN AND CO., LIMITED
ST. MARTIN'S STREET, LONDON
1924

TO

FREDDY

PREFACE

In *Forty-One Years in India*, my father described his life in that country, from the time he landed in Calcutta as a young subaltern to the day when he left Bombay at the age of sixty, having finished his work as Commander-in-Chief, a post he held for nearly eight years.

In that book he has given an account of the Mutiny of the Indian Army, and as a thread running through it is the story of the part he himself played in that struggle. But his object in writing was not so much to tell of his own doings as to record the gallant deeds and splendid fortitude of the small body of men, British and Indian, who by their valour saved India from relapsing into that state of unrest and misrule which, except perhaps for a brief period of good government under the enlightened ruler Akbar, had been the normal condition in which the peoples of India had lived for centuries.

He hoped, too, that by pointing out the

causes which led to the outbreak, and the lessons to be learnt, as he interpreted these by the light of his experience, he might be of assistance in preventing a recurrence of the disaster, and, above all, he wished to promote among his fellow-countrymen a more intimate knowledge and a better understanding of the Indian races and the Indian Army.

Since his death a packet of letters, labelled in his own handwriting "Letters written during the Mutiny by Fred. Roberts," has come to light. In these letters, thirty in number, is to be found the story of his personal experiences and adventures during the stirring days of 1857–58 as told to his father, mother, and sister. The first was written just as the earliest news of the disturbances at Meerut and Delhi reached him at Peshawar, and although it is evident that one or two are missing—not to be wondered at when the disturbed state of the country is borne in mind,—the majority reached their destination, and they tell their tale almost uninterruptedly to the day when he is able to give his family the joyful news that his leave has been sanctioned and that he is starting for home.

It is interesting to compare the letters with the book written many years later, when, in the calm of peace, my father looked back on his first campaign. It was but natural that a fuller knowledge should lead him to modify some of the criticisms of men and actions: criticisms written in the stir of strife, and when the first news, or rumours, of events reached him. Equally natural, too, that the expressions of antipathy to be found in the letters for the country in which he had witnessed and heard of the many dastardly crimes perpetrated by the mutineers, should give place to the terms of real affection in which he always speaks of India in his book, for he grew to love "the wonderful land of my adoption,"[1] and his love bred an understanding which gained him many a valued friendship. Rulers of states, landowners, stalwart men of the frontier, soldiers and sportsmen, he reckoned among his friends, and he gloried in the soldierly qualities of the Indian Army and the comradeship which exists between the British officers and their men. He never tired of telling of the tie between certain British and Indian regiments; the link forged on the Ridge before Delhi which binds the 60th Rifles and the 2nd Gurkhas; the friendship between the 72nd Highlanders (now the 1st Battalion Seaforth Highlanders) and 5th Royal Gurkhas, which sprang from their mutual support in many a fight in Afghanistan. Indian officers who

[1] From the Preface to *Forty-One Years in India.*

came to England were always welcomed to his home, and in the last year of his life nothing gave him greater pleasure than his appointment by the King to be Colonel-in-Chief of the Indian Expeditionary Force.

Frederick Sleigh Roberts was twenty-four years of age at the outbreak of the Mutiny. He came of a family which had been settled in Waterford for many generations. His great-grandfather, John Roberts, an architect to whom the city owes several of her public buildings, married a Miss Sautelle, the daughter of a Huguenot family which had fled to Ireland on the revocation of the Edict of Nantes. A considerable number of French refugees found their way to Waterford, and one of the oldest churches was given over to them. This church, now a ruin, is still known as the French Church, and, probably owing to their Huguenot connection, a considerable number of the Roberts family are buried in it.

John Roberts died in 1796. His son, the Reverend John Roberts, had a family of five sons and seven daughters, and of the sons three served their country in the Navy and Army. Two, Thomas and Samuel, rose to be Post-captains. Boys went out into the world at an early age in those days, and Samuel left his home when he was ten years old, and did not see it again, or have a day's leave, for twenty-one years. He fought in the wars against Spain and France, was wounded several times, and spent ten months in a Spanish dungeon in conditions so atrocious that only nine out of twenty-two survived the treatment they received. His services were rewarded with a knighthood and the Companionship of the Bath, and he retired to live in Waterford, "a crippled wreck," as he described himself.

Abraham Roberts, the fourth son, was born in 1784, and began his career in the Waterford Militia. This regiment was disbanded after the Peace of Amiens, when Abraham applied for a commission in the Line, and as there was some delay in his being gazetted he went to sea. In the course of his voyage he found himself at Calcutta, and, attracted by what he saw of life in India, he determined to make his career there. He was not deterred by finding on his return home that he had been posted to the 48th Foot,[1] and set to work to get a cadetship in the Service of the East India Company. He landed in Calcutta in 1805, and it is curious to read that he owed his seniority among his fellow-cadets to his having held a brief commission in the "Royal Army."

[1] Now the 1st Battalion Northamptonshire Regiment.

In the year young Abraham Roberts landed in India, Agra, Muttra, and Delhi marked the line of the "North-west Frontier"; when he left the country forty-eight years later, the frontier was approximately what it is to-day, and the last command he held was that of the Peshawar Division.

During that half-century he had his share of the work entailed by the gradual settlement of a vast area. He crossed the Sutlej with Lord Lake in pursuit of Holkar; saw service against the Pindaris and other predatory tribes in Bundelkund; in Sirmur and in the campaign against Nepal; played his part, as soldiers did in those days, in settling disputes between Hindus and Mahomedans, in forest work, and in the erection of new cantonments, and was one of the first people to build a house at Simla.

At the outbreak of the first Afghan War he commanded a brigade at the storming of Ghazni, and was in Kabul during the fateful months that preceded the disasters of 1842.[1] Of his

[1] The first Afghan War was undertaken to counteract Russian influence at Kabul, in the hope that the deposition of the Amir, Dost Mahomed, in favour of our nominee, Shah Shoojah, would achieve this end. It was proposed, after placing him on the throne, to withdraw our troops, leaving him to maintain his authority with the aid of a force composed of Hindustanis and Afghans raised for the purpose. Of this force Abraham Roberts was given the command. Shah Shoojah proved to be a mere puppet, incapable of governing his unruly subjects, and matters went from bad to worse, to culminate in the murder of our Envoy, and the disastrous retreat of our Army. From that prolonged agony one man out of fifteen thousand survived to tell the tale.

work there Sir William Napier wrote: "There was a General Roberts who commanded the Soojah's Force; he knew his business, he remonstrated against the false security of the Political Agents . . . he was laughed at, then insulted . . . wrote one or two dispatches to Lord Auckland pointing out these mischievous proceedings, and declaring that some great disaster would occur, demanded leave to return to India. He obtained it and left Cabul two months before the catastrophe, thus saving his honour and his life."[1] Roberts himself, when the news of the disaster he had predicted reached India, wrote: "I am not wiser than my neighbours, but where my suggestions in regard to precaution were neglected we have suffered. . . . I spoke the truth, and was thought an alarmist. Our rulers have much to answer for."

In 1830 Abraham Roberts[2] married the widow of Major Hamilton Maxwell, and on September 30, 1832, Frederick Sleigh Roberts was born at Cawnpore. Four years later, after a sojourn of thirty years in India, Colonel Roberts took his wife, small son, and daughter —the Harriet to whom many of the Mutiny

[1] *Life of General Sir William Napier, K.C.B.*, by H. A. Bruce.

[2] He had previously married Miss Ricketts, daughter of a Bengal civilian, who died in 1827.

letters are written—and his two stepchildren to England.

The story of the lives of most people connected with India is very similar. The necessities of education involve the early break-up of the family, and to the problem of bringing up children on limited means are added the anxieties and loneliness of long separations. Abraham Roberts and his wife were no exceptions to the rule; he went back to India, and she was left to struggle with the care of seven children—her own, and three of her husband's former marriage.

No letters written by Mrs. Roberts remain, but her husband kept abbreviated copies of the carefully numbered letters he wrote, and in the old book can be read not only the dates on which they were written and received, but the names of the ships in which they were sent, and they tell a story of deep affection, many anxieties, and the manifest strain of the long separation.

"I have been ailing, fear my complaint is a longing for home," he writes; and again, "I trust you and I shall not part again in this world after we meet, this absence is a sad thing and I am getting old." The expense of two households and a growing family causes much heart-searching: "You have had your share of anxiety and trouble, and I ought not to complain of mine." And in answer, apparently, to some comforting words from his wife: "I shall follow your sensible advice, and be no more annoyed at expense than cannot be avoided." In laying stress on the need for economy, he is careful to remind her to take care of herself: "Save what you can, but give yourself all you require, be vaccinated, run no risk, keep your beauty." And in answer to some letter showing worry and strain, he writes: "You must not talk of old age, I am told you look as young and beautiful as ever."

Association with India has its own recollections for childhood; "Good-byes" and "mail" letters loom largely, and Fred. Roberts has told of the children crowding round their mother to hear the letters read, and of how stories of Afghans and fighting were woven into his early memories of his father.

The boy, nicknamed by his sisters Sir Timothy Valliant, was small and delicate. While still in India he nearly died from an attack of brain-fever; and when he was given up by the doctors his father saved his life by resorting to a curious remedy. Recalling the practice of the hill-women, who when at work in the fields leave their babies by a stream and induce sleep by arranging for a gentle and continuous flow of water over their heads, he applied a similar soporific to his son; but the illness left its effect, for it deprived the boy of the sight of his right eye.

Mrs. Roberts was evidently a woman of character and intelligence, and in after-life her son recalled the anxious thought she gave to his education, and how greatly he had profited by her choice of the school to which she sent him. This was at Hampton, kept by a Mr. Mills, who had been a master in the Navy, and his pupil was wont to declare that his system was an excellent one for the training of mind and body, and that the weekly option he gave misdemeanants of a long punishment task or a sound flogging was inspired by a desire to develop character and a capacity for quick decision.

It was the mother's wish to send her son to Eton, but the possibility of being able to do this depended, apparently, on Abraham Roberts getting command of a regiment. "What is the expense of Eton?" he writes. "I should like Freddy to go there, if I had a regiment I should not mind, but at present I burn the candle at both ends." Promotion in the East India Company's Service went by seniority, and the father notes sadly that there are seventeen ahead of him, and with the quaint comment, "I wish for no man's death, but with all between me and a regiment," evidently thought he might have to wait some time.

Mrs. Roberts got her wish, and Freddy was sent to Eton in 1845.

There is much talk in the letters on the boy's future career. "From all you say I shall be proud of Freddy." "Freddy will remain at home, Church or law." "If Freddy is clever I hope he will not think of the Army." "Freddy must be Lord Chancellor," are some of the references, while the mother fondly hoped he would go to Oxford or Cambridge, and enter the Church. Meanwhile the object of all this thought had decided for himself. In a short memorandum he has written, "I had quite made up my mind to be a soldier, I had never thought of any other profession"; and he got his wish.

Failing in an attempt to get him appointed to the East India Company's Service, his father sent him to Sandhurst at the age of fourteen, and the boy records that to his great surprise he came out second in the entrance examination.

He was not destined, however, to join the Queen's Service at the commencement of his career, for, no doubt from financial considerations, his father again applied to the Directors of the East India Company, this time with success. That the proposed change was not altogether welcome is shown by a letter to his father in October 1848, when apparently the choice of a profession was once more under consideration.

"Many thanks for your very kind letter and also for the sovereign which I received yesterday. I will try and make it last as long as possible. Some time ago my dearest Father I decided on the Army as the profession I should like the best, and would certainly prefer the Queen's Service to going to India, but still as you say in the Queen's Service I may go to India for a number of years, and then come home and be put on half-pay. I do not think I should like the Church or the law—Civil Engineering is the only (one?) but if you and Mamma think I should not be able to get on, I would not for anything be in it. Do write me a line my dearest Father and tell me yours and dearest Mamma's wishes, it will certainly be my own fault if I am not happy in whatever profession I enter for. I am sure no son had ever more choice or a kinder Father and Mother in wishing to gratify him. If you and Mamma wish me to go to Addiscombe[1] I will go there

[1] Addiscombe was the military training college for the East India Company's Army. The cadets who passed out highest were given their choice of joining the Engineers and Artillery.

willingly, and after all the advantages you have given me by the best education I should be ashamed of myself were I not to get the Engineers. . . . I am very sorry my writing has not been so good lately, but I will try and improve. Hoping to hear from you soon, believe me to remain, my dearest Father, with best love to all—Your ever affect. and fond son,

"FREDERICK SLEIGH ROBERTS."

Fred. Roberts went to Addiscombe, and was promised by his father a hundred pounds and a gold watch if he passed into the Engineers, and fifty pounds with the watch if he succeeded in getting into the Artillery. The father's own struggles and difficulties no doubt prompted him to offer this stimulant to his son to work for the better-paid Corps. It was to the boy's own satisfaction, as will be seen in the letters written before Delhi, that he became a gunner. He received from his father the gold watch, and in the fifty pounds the only money he did not earn for himself.

In February 1852 he sailed for India; in his farewell letter from Southampton to his mother, whom he did not expect to see for ten years, he wrote: "I am now indeed away from your kind care, and entirely depending on myself for all my future actions, a fact which I can hardly realise, but I will ever remember your few last words to me, and when in any difficulty think of you, and with God's blessing I shall succeed."

ROBERTS.

Nov. 1923.

NOTE

In the following letters, written to people familiar with India and the organisation of the Army in that country, the allusions and abbreviations may be puzzling to the general reader; it would, perhaps, be well, therefore, to state briefly what was the composition of the Army at the outbreak of the Mutiny.

Then, as now, there were a certain number of regiments, Cavalry and Infantry, of the British Army serving in India for a limited number of years; these were usually referred to as "Royal," or "Queen's" troops: but by far the greater part of the Army was in the pay of the Honourable East India Company, and consisted of all arms.

A small proportion were white soldiers, generally designated Europeans; the remainder were natives of India, serving under British officers. In the Artillery there was a preponderance of Europeans, but there were none in the Cavalry, and in Northern India there were only three regiments of European Infantry.

The Company's Bengal Army—a designation which covered the whole of Northern India, as distinct from Madras and Bombay—consisted of "regular" troops, raised between the years 1757 and 1825, and recruited from Oudh and the parts of the country which had long been under our rule; these were the men who became disaffected in 1857. The Company had also a considerable body of "irregular" troops, a portion of whom joined the mutineers; some local corps, and regiments of Gurkhas; and, in addition, the Punjab Irregular Force. This Force had been called into being by the recent acquisitions of the Punjab and Scinde, and the consequent propinquity to the wild tribesmen of the frontier, and it was recruited from among the martial races of the North-west. These regiments remained true to their salt, and under the leadership of the keen young British officers, to whom the adventurous life on the frontier made appeal, gave magnificent service in the Mutiny, as they have done ever since.

R.

ILLUSTRATIONS

LETTERS WRITTEN DURING THE INDIAN MUTINY

PESHAWUR,
May 14th, 1857.

MY DEAREST MOTHER—When you hear all the rows and disturbances that are going on in this country, you will be anxious, I am sure, to hear how we are prospering at Peshawur. At present all has gone well, and I am not very sure but that we are better off in the Punjab than elsewhere. From Delhi and Meerut we hear strange accounts, all of which you will, of course, hear about in more detail than I can give, as, at present, we know nothing but what a short electric telegraph message could convey, the wires having been cut soon after, all communication is cut off. Yesterday news came from Lahore that the Native Infantry had been disarmed. A Council of War was held here when it was decided to separate the N. Infantry here, sending them to the different Forts and Outposts where they can't do much harm, and despatching a force at once towards Jhelum, consisting of a troop of H.A.,[1] two Queen's Corps and some Irregular Infantry and Cavalry, to assemble at Jhelum and act whenever occasion may require. The troops are now all in motion. The General[2] goes off by dâk[3] this evening to join the Chief Commissioner[4] at Pindee or Jhelum. I ride down on Saturday and Sunday, and then, of course, our movements depend on circumstances. I am in high glee at the thoughts of service, but most sincerely wish it were in a better cause, and not against our own soldiers. All confidence in the native Army is at an end, and the most decided measures and strenuous exertions will only save India now. We have some good men on this Frontier—Edwardes, Nicholson, Cotton, Chamberlain, etc. Old Reed I don't think much of—he has one good quality, namely: listening to reason—which is better than being obstinate, when ability is not combined. My servants and traps went off last night. When you receive this, dearest Mother, I hope all will have been settled. I would anticipate no very great calamity were every Division of the Army as well off for sensible heads as this is, but

[1] Horse Artillery.

[2] Major-General Reed, commanding the Peshawur Division.

[3] A post or establishment for the conveyance of letters and travellers; from the Hindi *dāk*, a post.

[4] Sir John Lawrence, Chief Commissioner of the Punjab, afterwards Lord Lawrence, and Governor-General of India.

some of our older Officers are perfect children—quite unable to take care of themselves. The weather is hot now for a Campaign, but the Troops are in better health than at the end of the hot weather, and I don't think heat does one much harm if one has no time to think about it and get restless. My plans are to go to Pindee with old Reed, and then join the movable Column wherever it may go. I'll work hard, and I have no doubt get on. Dear, darling Mother, I feel such love for you, just as if I had never left you for half an hour. Don't be alarmed or frightened when you read all the accounts, or should you not hear from me regularly, I'll write whenever I can. It is just possible everything may be settled down country ere this. Up here, of course, we can't hear, and it is wise to take every precaution. How jolly you must all be, and so am I, Mother dear. We had a grand Masons' Ball the other evening—the very best party of the season. The W.M. [1] proposed the Ladies!! in no end of an eloquent speech. A young fellow of my Regiment has just come from England with a wife, his name is Cookes, and hers was Morris, from Waterford. She does not know any of you personally, although the Edward Roberts she is well acquainted with. She

[1] The Writer.

seems rather nice. The Boisragons have left Pindee and gone to Simla, where he has got a new appointment. Isn't it disgusting they should have left just as I am going down. Maggie is such a nice little girl, and I could have been very happy with them. I am very busy, so good-bye, dearest Mother. With kind love to the General, Harrie, Hamilton and Innes.[1]—Believe me, your very affectionate son,

FRED. ROBERTS.

RAWUL PINDEE,
May 21st, 1857.

MY DEAREST MOTHER—I have only time for a few lines just to tell you how jolly I am, and to ask after you all. This letter is going in an Express to the Bombay Government, so I hope you will receive it. I wrote a few lines the last Mail from Peshawur which have probably never reached you, owing to the disturbed state of the country—horrible blackguards these Sepoys,[2] are they not? The Mutiny has not gained ground, and it is, thank God, only amongst the soldiers. If the country were to rise, we should have to hold our own in different parts of the dominion, pending the arrival of reinforcements, and, of course, sacrificing all the *tame* stations. I do

[1] His father, his sister Harriet, and his half-brother and sister.

[2] Native soldiers, from the Persian *sipahi*, from *sipah*, an army soldiery.

not anticipate such a thing, but we have a most dilatory undecided Commander-in-Chief.[1] John Lawrence has done wonders in the Punjab. The Native Infantry Regts. are being all separated, and Irregulars from the Derajât are coming rapidly into these parts. A large force under Chamberlain assembles at Wuzeer-abad, of which *I am going as Quartermaster-General*![2] Hurrah!!! All the troops are in motion, and I leave for Jhelum to-morrow morning to make arrangements about ferries over all the Rivers between this and Lahore. Unless matters get quiet, we shall see Delhi. Chamberlain is determined to push on, but the heat will be so fearful, that if our men get very sickly, it will stop us materially. I am in capital health, and sincerely hope I may keep so, then I think Quartermaster-General's Department is pretty certain!! eh, My own darling Mother. I have no time for more, from Jhelum you shall hear if I have time. God bless you all.

With kind love, ever your affectionate son,

FRED. ROBERTS.

[1] General the Hon. George Anson. In *Forty-One Years in India*, Lord Roberts describes the steps taken by the Commander-in-Chief, and says: "There was no hesitation on General Anson's part, or delay in issuing the necessary orders."

[2] In 1857 the Staff system of the Army was similar to that in force in the days of Wellington. The Quartermaster-General's Department was responsible for Operations and Intelligence, and performed the duties now carried out by the General Staff. The system was changed in 1888.

CAMP NEAR JHELUM,
May 22nd, 1857.

MY DEAREST FATHER—I am sure you have been astonished at the news the last two mails must have taken home—the mutiny of the Sepoys all thought so faithful and true, nasty scoundrels. They have shown themselves at heart to be worse than even our enemies. No Sikh or Afghan ever abused and killed our women and children as these wretches have done. The papers, of course, give you an account of all that goes on, so I will confine myself to the details of the Punjab affairs, and a summary of the mutiny in general. The 19th N.I. were disbanded, as you will have read, for gross mutiny, but our imbecile Government, instead of treating the men as mutineers, paid them up, let them keep their *uniforms*!! and saw them safely across the river. The General Officer, poor fellow!! on reading the order to dismiss them shed tears!! The cartridges have been, I believe, at the bottom of the whole affair, and that a general rise was anticipated and preconcerted by the Native Army there is little doubt of, the 19th being too precipitous in commencing. Well, affairs went on. The 39th[1] became as bad as the 19th N.I., when, on the

[1] The writer probably intended to write 34th. The 34th N.I., stationed at Barrackpore, was reported to be disaffected in February 1857; an outbreak occurred in March, and the regiment was disbanded. See p. 23, note.

General Abraham Roberts C.B.

From a photograph

evening of the 11th inst., one of our Officers at Mess received a telegraphic message from Delhi that the Sepoys had mutinied and were killing all the inhabitants and burning the cantonments. The next day, a similar message came from Meerut, when a Council of War was held, and it was determined to act independently in the Punjab; imagining, and very truly as it has turned out, that the Commander-in-Chief would have enough to do below, old Reed took command of the whole (the Council consisted of Edwardes,[1] Chamberlain,[2] Nicholson[3] (about the best man in India), Brig. Cotton,[4] and General Reed. Wright, the Deputy-Assistant-Adjutant-General, and myself being present), and orders were sent at once for N.I. Regiments from different stations in the Punjab to march into the Derajât, and some of the Punjab Force, on whom we can, I believe, rely, to come into the Punjab, it was further decided that a movable column should assemble at Jhelum (subsequently removed to Wuzeerabad) to act wherever occasion should require. General Reed was also recommended to proceed to R. Pindee, so as to be in direct communication with John Lawrence. On the 16th, I left Peshawur and reached Pindee the

[1] Afterwards Major-General Sir Herbert Edwardes, K.C.B.
[2] Afterwards Field-Marshal Sir Neville Chamberlain, G.C.B.
[3] Brigadier John Nicholson, C.B.
[4] Afterwards General Sir Sydney Cotton, G.C.B.

next day. By this time, the Commander-in-Chief had reached Umballa and was making arrangements for an advance on Delhi, where the mutineers are fortifying themselves, but Government, since you left the country, to save a few rupees have sold all the camels they had, and trusted to contractors. The consequence is none are forthcoming, and the Umballa force can't move. At Meerut, they seem panic-stricken. From the first they only had 2 N.I. Regiments and one Cavalry Corps, to meet which they had the Carabineers, 60th Rifles, 1 Troop and 1 Battery of European Artillery Men, and some 300 Artillery recruits, yet, can you believe it, they have entrenched themselves and never stir out; although I hear there is no enemy near them, the C. in Chief at Umballa has allowed the 2 N.I. Regiments there to do all but open mutiny. At Jullundhur the same thing is going on, and all the ladies are sent to sleep in the European Artillery Barracks where they frighten each other to death with stories. At Ferozepore the 45th and 57th broke out, the latter eventually gave themselves up and were disarmed, but the other Regiment before making off burnt nearly the whole station down, and this in the face of an European Battery of Artillery and the 61st Queen's,[1] besides the 10th Cavalry who remained

[1] Now the 2nd Battalion Gloucestershire Regiment.

loyal. Maltby, the padre, whom you remember at Peshawur, writes from Ferozepore—"such cowards as the mutineers I never saw. I saved my own house by remaining in it. They were afraid to come near, and took 3 shots at me, and had I only 50 Europeans, I could have cleared the whole place." At Lahore, they heard the men intended mutinying and disarmed them. Several of the Sepoys have since run away. Sialkot and upwards to Peshawur have hitherto kept quiet, but letters have been intercepted, which plainly show the whole Army is more or less disaffected. At Peshawur, the Regiment most suspected, the 64th (the one Uncle Hunter[1] dealt with so summarily in Scinde) were marched across the Cabul river into the Forts, and there they can do what they like, the very worst will be to kill their own Officers, but not a Sepoy would escape, all the Ferries are guarded, and the Bridge of Boats at Attock is taken down, a wing of Europeans being placed in the Fort, the same with Peshawur. I anticipate nothing serious there

[1] Major-General George Hunter, C.B. He married a sister of Mrs. Roberts. He was commanding in Upper Scinde when the 64th Native Infantry mutinied in 1844 on a question of pay. His promptitude in dealing with the situation was criticised, in the first instance, by the Adjutant-General, but met with the approval of Sir Charles Napier, the Governor of Scinde, and of Lord Ellenborough, the Governor-General. Writing to the latter, General Hunter's comment on the criticism was: "I have yet to learn after forty-three years' service that the first moment of a mutiny is not the proper time to interfere and put it down."

on this account; but it is too disgusting to see the insane things Officers do—enough to ruin any Army, and the craven-hearted fellows seem to think they have nothing to do but make up stories and frighten the poor women out of their wits.[1] However, please God this state of affairs will not last long. The Column will be assembled at Wuzeerabad by the next week, and then I fancy we shall march down country to assist at Delhi, if necessary, and coerce all the unruly Regiments on the way. For the business a better man than Chamberlain could not be found, and am I not a lucky fellow going on his Staff; Inshallah,[2] I'll be mentioned in Orders and get into the Department permanently.

26th May, JHELUM.—I have been unable to finish this before. I had to hurry off from Rawul Pindee, and have been hard at work ever since getting the troops over the Jhelum and Chenab. All are now in motion on Lahore, and I leave this evening for Wuzeerabad with Chamberlain in the Mail Cart. We shall then push on to Lahore, and farther, if necessary. Since I

[1] In the chapter headed "What brought about the Mutiny?" Lord Roberts in his book comments on the Army of the East India Company, and points out the causes which, in his opinion, resulted in a want of efficiency among some of the officers.

[2] If God wills; from the Persian, *in*, if; *sha*, wills; *Allah*, God.

commenced this, 4 Regiments in Peshawur have been disarmed, 3 N.I., and the 5th Lt. Cavalry. Another N.I., the 55th, are at *Murdan* in Eusofzaie, and we are anxiously looking out for news, as these are in mutiny and a force had been sent with orders to slay every man unless the ringleader were given up. However, we shall know to-day. The Gerrards are here with their Regiment, the 14th. It seems less disaffected than others, and will, I think, do their duty quietly as long as they are left alone. The natives have all sorts of ideas in their heads, the chief one that we want to convert them, another is intense dislike to the C. in Chief! Up till the present time, the following Corps have mutinied more or less:—5th, 9th, 11th, 16th, 19th, 20th, 24th, 26th, 27th, 34th, 36th, 38th, 45th, 51st, 54th, 55th, 57th, 60th, 61st, 64th; 3rd Cavalry, 8th Do., 5th Do. Disbanding most of these when the work is over will be a good thing, and forming European Regiments in their places. I am glad to say no Artillery have behaved badly as yet, altho' almost all the Sappers have.

You must give this to Harrie to read for you, as I am afraid it is not very neat nor legible, but I have nothing with me, not even a spare shirt. The Gerrards join in much love, and believe me, dearest Father, ever your very affect. son,

FRED. ROBERTS.

Notwithstanding the heat, I am as jolly and well as possible.

CAMP AMRITSUR,
June 11th, 1857.

MY DEAREST MOTHER—I have no doubt you will be anxiously looking out for news from me, so I'll set to work early and give you a long letter. I last wrote from Rawul Pindee, I think, a few hurried lines sent by Express to Bombay, which I hope you have received. You will have heard by that of my being well and happy, and appointed by Chamberlain as Staff of the movable Column. Well the troops assembled at Jhelum, and we have come along this far, doing a little business on the road such as disarming Regiments and executing mutineers. The death that seems to have the most effect is being blown from a gun. It is rather a horrible sight, but in these times we cannot be particular. Drum Head Courts-Martial are the order of the day in every station, and had they begun this régime a little earlier, one half of the destruction and mutiny would have been saved. Oh, my dear Mother, you would not believe men and Englishmen could ever have been guilty of such imbecility as has almost invariably been displayed during this crisis, some few have shone, but they are exceptions. In Peshawur, fortunately, sensible, firm fellows were at the head of affairs, or I dread to think what would have been the result. What I wanted was to get the women out of the valley. Some advocated this move when Colonel Mackeson[1] was murdered, but only the timid ones. However, our situation lately has been very different. Mutiny in one's own Camp is difficult to deal with; and then the rascals have treated all the poor women and children so horribly when they had a chance. Fortunately, the crisis at Peshawur is over, and they can now hold their own, I trust. At Jullundhur they should, and deserve really to have been all murdered, I mean those in authority. They would positively believe nothing except the *fidelity* of the Native Troops. Over and over again they had warnings. From Lahore, even, I wrote to them what was going on, and even when the men did mutiny and were consulting about attacking the guns, Brigadier Johnstone would not allow them to fire. Isn't it horrible, Mother dear? Very nearly the whole of one Regiment could have been blown to pieces, instead of which they got off and cut up several Officers. None died, I believe, but many are

[1] Commissioner of Peshawur. He was murdered by a religious fanatic in 1853.

badly wounded. Poor little Maggie Boisragon was there alone, her husband being away with his Regiment and she got a bad fright. However, in this country, the women are the only ones who have behaved properly. The men are positively disgusting, and make one ashamed of being a man. Should the Column have a chance under our present leader, Chamberlain, I don't think it would do badly, but I am afraid there is not much chance. We are going on to Jullundhur, but our movements, of course, depend on what takes place at Delhi. We have heard of the commencement of the fight but they were at it still when the Cassid[1] left. I wish to Goodness I were down there. However, we are sure of some fun in Peshawur this cold weather. One Regiment, the 55th N.I., have gone over almost bodily into Swat (13th June), and they will, I have no doubt, trouble us eventually. An express has just come for more European troops to be sent to Delhi, the 8th[2] from Jullundhur go, and we move on to-night towards Jullundhur. There, I hope to have the European Infantry and push on down country with the Artillery and Cavalry. It is a bad sign their wanting more troops at Delhi, for if they do not succeed in taking the place

[1] A Persian word, *Qāsid*, a messenger.
[2] Now the King's (Liverpool Regiment).

before the Regiments can arrive, I am afraid it will be a bad business. This has been a queer season certainly, I have not slept under a punkah[1] once this year, and very seldom have a chance of one in the day time, and, strange to say, I never felt better, and never remember thinking less about the heat. When the rains come, our men will, I am afraid, suffer from the exposure, but hitherto, the weather has been most propitious. Something has happened to the English letters, I have not received a line since April 30th, nearly two months, nor have we had any English news later than the 24th March. I long to hear again from you, my own dear Mother. It will be some time before the country gets quiet, and our dâks will always run a risk. However, it will be very unlucky if all the English Mails are robbed. You would scarcely believe how paralysed everything is. A letter from Calcutta is considered an extraordinary affair, and every day we hear of fresh Regiments mutinying. I think 35 are gone altogether, besides some 30 more who have been disarmed and are ready to go. Perfectly ridiculous, an Army going to pieces in this way. I only hope they will all go and that we may never have another Poorbea[2] Sepoy again. Up to the present, the Native

[1] A Hindi word meaning "fan."

[2] The term applied to men recruited from Oudh and other districts in the eastern parts of Northern India. From *purb*, east.

Artillery have behaved well. Only two Batteries have gone, and they were both seized by the N. Infantry. I hope, however, that they will never have more Native Artillery, nothing but Europeans for guns should be allowed. I believe I am promoted in the room of some of the poor fellows who have lost their lives by these gallant *Sepoys*! but I would far rather remain a 2nd Lieut. all my life than rise through such horrid means. Up to the present moment, we don't know exactly who were killed in Delhi, or who escaped, and I am in hopes that some may even yet be found in the City, who have been taken care of by the natives. I can't believe all would be such blackguards, they are tolerable monsters certainly. A man (a native) who was at Delhi during the massacre told me he saw 8 ladies let out, and shot one after the other, they nearly all had children with them, who were killed before their eyes. So I don't think Poorbea Sepoys deserve much pity, nor do they find it. The day before yesterday 40 belonging *to one Regt.*, including native Officers, etc., were blown away from guns in Peshawur, and this fate awaits many yet I trust. I feel so happy to think, dearest Mother, all those I care about are at home. It would be horrible to have any one you loved in this country, and if anything has ever helped to keep me from marrying this mutiny has, as it is only myself, I care little where I go, and only want to be in a scrimmage somewhere. But I really pity poor fellows who leave wives behind them, for one station may be as bad as another if the war continues. As long as the country people remain quiet, we can manage the native Army, but should the sound of "religion" stir them up, we should have a little fighting. However, except in one or two districts, they have behaved well. I have plenty of work. Chamberlain has no other staff, and I am Quartermaster-General! Brigade Major!! and, until yesterday, Commissariat Officer!!! The General would, I am sure, be amused and astonished seeing me at the desk all day, writing, writing incessantly. However, I get on pretty well, the only part that bothers me is not getting sleep at night. I am always obliged to be first on the ground to pitch the camp. With a large force, this is sometimes difficult, and I generally snooze on the ground beside my horse. On "halts" I take it out, which makes up.

Now, my dearest Mother, I must end. Write to me every Mail nice long letters, and tell me you are happy and well, and that dear little Harriet and the General do not suffer. Give my best love to them all, also dear Innes, John,[1]

[1] Captain John Sherston. He married Innes Maxwell, Fred. Roberts' half-sister.

Hamilton and *Capt. and Mrs. G. Roberts*,[1] and believe me, my own dearly beloved mother, your very affect. son,

FRED. ROBERTS.

CAMP BEFORE DELHI,
June 29th, 1857.

MY DEAREST MOTHER—Here I am at the right place at last you see, which will astonish you not a little, I have no doubt. I wrote to you last from Jullundhur, since which the movable Column marched to the banks of the Sutlej. There we disarmed the 2 N.I. Corps with us, and the Column was ordered to return towards Lahore. I thought it a pity to go back after having come so far, so I asked Nicholson, who had succeeded Chamberlain, to allow me to go on. He answered, "Well, Roberts, your loss I can't replace, both personally and publicly I regret your going, but, at the same time you have more chance of getting on before Delhi." So off I started with saddle and tooth-brush on the top of the Mail Cart and was not long in arriving here. I fully expected being kicked out of the Staff and sent to duty with the Artillery, and was not a little agreeably surprised when I was offered two appointments, one Quartermaster-General with the Cavalry

[1] George Roberts, a half-brother, had lately married.

Brigade, and the other Deputy-Assistant-*Adjutant*-General under Sir H. Barnard.[1] Well, I chose the former, being in my own line. *All* the Artillery Captains, imagining I was joining the Corps again, asked for me for their troops, so I felt quite proud. Dear mother, you don't think I am conceited telling you all this. I know it will please you, the General and dear little Harriet, to hear such good news, and I feel anything but conceit dearest, only wondering at my luck in getting on so well. This morning, I received dear Harriet's letter of the 1st of May. The 20th April has never turned up. Do write to me every Mail, Mother, because I may not receive your letters, should you only write now and then. Delhi is not taken yet, it is very much more formidable than people think. The last of our reinforcements will arrive in a few days, and unless we intend remaining here for 6 months, we must go at it at once. I am so glad, Mother, I am here, and in such a good position. Since my arrival yesterday morning, nothing has gone on, but a few shot and shell exchanged. I will write to you every Mail, Mother dear. To-day I cannot give you a long letter, if possible I'll finish it to-morrow, should I not, it will be

[1] The command of the Delhi Field Force devolved on Major-General Sir Henry Barnard on the death of General Anson.

for want of time. God bless you all.—Ever your own affect. son,

FRED. ROBERTS.

30th June.—We were awoke this morning by the alarm, and have been on the *qui vive* for some hours. However, the firing is ceasing and the few enemy that came out are retiring, so there won't be much to-day. Good-bye again, Mother.—Your affect. son,

FRED. ROBERTS.

CAMP BEFORE DELHI,
July 23rd, 1857.

MY DEAREST MOTHER—How time passes. Nearly the day for English letters to go off again. I hope you received the letter I wrote to you from this on the 12th,[1] and that no news from Lahore later than the 10th reached you by the last Mail, as you will not then have heard of my having been wounded until a day or two perhaps ere you receive this, or the few lines I scribbled to the General on the 15th,[1] and which I scarcely expected would leave by the last Mail. I merely wrote them on the chance. However, in case they may have been lost, I will continue my story from the 13th. That day we were quiet but early on the 14th,

[1] Missing.

the enemy attacked, as usual, our front and right. During the forenoon they were allowed to expend their ammunition firing on our Piquets and nothing very particular took place. Once while the General and Staff were standing by the Battery on our right a party of Cavalry appeared on the road behind our Piquet. Having some irregular Cavalry in our own Camp, it was doubtful who these fellows were, so the guns were ordered not to fire, and I, perceiving what was wanted, volunteered to find out who our friends were, unfortunately, as it turned out afterwards. The only Cavalry near at hand that I could take with me were some twenty Sowars[1] belonging to a Native Pensioner of Government—an Afghan by the bye named "Jan Fishan Khan," perhaps the General may remember him. So, getting this rabble together, I started off and soon came to the place where I thought the men had appeared, sending videttes on ahead was all nonsense with the men I had with me, for I knew, unless I went first, not a soul would go on, so I turned up the road leading thro' a village in ruins, and came on 3 or 4 Sowars and 2 or 3 Infantry. These fellows ran away the instant they saw me. I galloped after them, and the next turn in the Road found myself in front of a large party

[1] Native cavalry soldiers; from the Persian, *sawar*, a horseman.

of the enemy's cavalry, who were out reconnoitring. I knew they always ran when they were attacked, and altho' about 3 times as strong as my party, I thought we would have a go at them, but when I turned round, I found, except the old native, his nephew and one or two men, all the rest had bolted and were firing off their matchlocks in all directions. This disgusted me not a little, as I had to turn quietly round and retire. However, I found out the fellows, and with their usual pluck, altho' I walked away, they never attempted to follow up and only showed themselves in twos and threes the rest of the morning. Well, about 3.0 P.M., a force consisting of 6 H.A. guns, 300 of the 1st Fusiliers[1] and a Punjab Infantry Corps, was ordered to drive the enemy back to the City, and I was sent with it. The enemy had brought some field guns out with them, and while we were standing in the road, a round shot came and knocked 2 or 3 of the 1st Fusiliers over. The Infantry then sent out skirmishers on both sides (I think I described the ground before to you, a kind of suburb called "Subjhee Mundee,"[2] consisting of houses now in ruins, high walls, gardens, etc., the very best place for an enemy, and only one or two roads down

[1] The 1st European Bengal Fusiliers; afterwards the Royal Munster Fusiliers.

[2] *Subzi Mandi*, Persian for Vegetable Market.

which guns could go). Well, on we went, slowly, fierce fighting, until a body of "Pandies"[1] appeared on the road. The guns came into action when the fellows fled, and Chamberlain calling to me to go with him, galloped to bring the skirmishers round upon them. We had some difficulty about this. Men do not like advancing from cover when they are being pitched into by a heavy fire from some unseen enemy. We could see the rascals from being mounted, and after halloaing on the men, got them to make a rush. This was the jolly old Fusiliers; the Officer with them, Daniell, had gone to the rear wounded, so it was lucky we went that way. There is no doubt about Chamberlain being a dashing, gallant fellow. Wherever the fire was hottest there he was sure to be, and I, thinking his invitation to go along with him was perhaps intended for the rest of the day, did not like leaving him. Well, we had got back on the road by this time, and down came a couple of H.A. guns to clear the road in front. They came into action just where the trunk road branches into the open near the City Walls, but were of very little use.

[1] The mutineers came to be known by the name of a sepoy of the 34th Native Infantry, Mungal Pandy, who was the first insurgent to be executed. He attacked and wounded the Adjutant and Sergeant-Major of his regiment, and a Court composed of Indian officers unanimously found him guilty.

The guns from the heavy Batteries pitched in, shot, shell, grape, etc., and we were within nice musketry range of the Pandy Infantry, who scattering about the open, could not be damaged much by our two light pieces. The consequence was the gunners were knocked over right and left. Seeing a Howitzer almost disabled for want of men, I dismounted, remembering that, altho' on the Staff, I was a "gunner," and set to work. However, we were soon ordered to retire, and the word to "limber up" was given. I got on my horse again, and turning round to look after the horses in the limbers, who were very unsteady from the firing, I got shot in the back, just where my waistbelt goes. Most fortunately, thro' God's mercy, I had a small leather pouch on my belt. The bullet went just thro' the middle of this, thro' my trousers and shirt, and made a small hole in my back. I can scarcely describe the feeling I had, Mother dear. Altho' we could not, I believe, have been under a heavier fire (9 men besides myself and Thompson, who was the Officer with the other gun, were knocked over in a few minutes out of 2 guns' crews) from the excitement, I suppose, I quite forgot about the chance of being hit, and when I got this awful crack on my back for a second did not know what it was. Feeling a little faint, I dismounted. Wriford of the

Fusiliers, thinking I was mortally wounded, sent a couple of men to take hold of me. However, after getting a glass of water, I thought I could ride, and was not so very much hurt after all, so I mounted and rode alongside of the guns to the rear. There is little doubt what the result would have been had I not had the pouch on. As it is, I am nearly well, and but for the damp weather, would probably have been so, but at this time of the year, wounds are difficult to heal, and mine is discharging a great deal more than I expected. Fortunately, the ball just missed the spine, so I suffer hardly any pain. Am I not a lucky fellow my own Mother, and has not God been merciful to me, I can never be sufficiently thankful. We suffered a good deal on the 14th, about 200 men killed and wounded, besides some 14 Officers, Chamberlain very badly in the left arm. The Pandies must have had several killed, but they have come out almost every day since, not staying long, retiring after bothering our Piquets a short time. However, to-day they attacked our left Front, but were beaten back. Our loss was small, except in Officers. It must be luck I think. I can scarcely imagine, in the row and noise that takes place, they could pick off Officers. Artillery again suffered the most —3 Officers out of 5 wounded, one I fear is likely to lose his leg. Guns are little or no use in these scrimmages. The roads are so narrow they can scarcely turn round, and are, I think, in the way, except perhaps for the moral effect.

24th.—All quiet to-day. Nothing but rain. Poor Tommy Greensill[1] was killed in such a sad way a few days ago. He was attached to the Engineers, and one evening had been out with a party clearing the jungle in front of a piquet. When his time was up, they all returned; Tommy and 2 or 3 other Officers began talking about a mine the enemy were said to be driving, and agreed to go and see if they could find it out. After walking a little distance, they came to a ravine. Tommy went with 9 men of the 75th[2] Queen's into the ravine, while the other two Officers walked along the top. They agreed to signal to each other by whistling. After walking along Tommy found his whistle was not answered, so taking one of the men with him and telling the others to halt, he scrambled up the side of the ravine and appeared suddenly a few yards in front of the two other Officers, seeing something white, they called out, thinking it was one of the enemy, and getting no answer, called again. Still no answer,

[1] A cousin. [2] Now the 1st Battalion Gordon Highlanders.

when one of them fired. The ball passed right thro' poor Tom and wounded the man who was with him, and who, strange to say, was so completely behind Tom, the Officers never saw him. Thinking this was probably the first "Pandy" of many, the 2 Officers ran down to where they supposed Greensill would be, and said, "look out, here are the enemy." The men replied, "where is Capt. Greensill?" It then flashed across them what had happened, and rushing up, they found Tom mortally wounded. This was about 8½ P.M. Tom was carried home and died at 1.0 in the morning. He was sensible to the last and made his Will, leaving all to his 2 children. I heard nothing of it till all was over. The graveyard is immediately by my tent, so I was able to toddle that far and attend the poor fellow's funeral. So sad losing a life in such a way. What with being killed, dying of wounds and cholera, we have already a melancholy long list. I will write to Uncle Greensill and tell him the bad news, a task I dislike very much, but it must be done. However, I think, Mother dear, this business has passed the turn. From various reports, we hear that several Regiments are between Cawnpore and Agra. Once they arrive, Delhi will fall, and then several columns will be formed to go about the country. We are perfectly in the dark even now what has taken place below Agra, and I positively dread to hear. One does not mind Officers being killed so much, it is more or less expected to be the fate of soldiers, but these poor women and children—it makes one's very blood run cold to think what they have suffered. I only trust the ruffians have had the mercy to kill those that have fallen into their hands and not taken them with them, as we hear some have done. Such atrocities have never, I fancy, been so universally committed. Our enemies, the Afghans and Sikhs respected our wives and children, but these cowardly wretches delight in torturing them, and yet I'll venture to say the English papers and Members of Parliament will try to excuse them and put the blame on every one else but the proper scoundrels. Don't think I am in low spirits, darling Mother, writing as I do, very far from it. I could not be jollier. Plenty of nice men of my Regiment whom I know intimately, a capital Mess (as Messes go, but I really believe in three weeks, there will be scarcely a bottle of beer and wine in the whole camp), besides meeting no end of old friends; and then my position for so young an Officer, in fact I could not be better off, and I have got just what I wanted in the Quartermaster-General's Department on service, and service that I enjoy most thoroughly—as far as the results go, helping to exterminate every Sepoy in the Army; but this hanging about Delhi is very disheartening to the men, constant, almost daily, alarms and scrimmages, often under arms the whole day. At this time of the year this is very trying. However, that would be nothing if we had a good fight and done with it, but these Pandies are innumerable and never become less, and we go pottering about perfectly aware that we can do nothing else. However, please God before I write again, I shall have ridden thro' Delhi, and then I hope to join some Force going either towards Rohilkund, and Oude or Gwalior—all new countries to me, and all of which I am very anxious to see; and then, if I may look so far, after the fun is over, to return to Peshawur permanent in the Department. Won't that be nice, my Mother. I am afraid, according to the new rules, Brevets can't be promised to Subalterns as formerly, but there are plenty of other rewards, and what I want more than any other is the *Victoria Cross*. Oh! if I can only manage that, how jolly I should be. I shall send this off to-morrow to Maggie Boisragon to Lahore. I shall be sure then of its going, and the last safe day I will write a few lines just to say how I am getting on, for I know you will be very anxious, dear Mother. I shall long to hear about Innes and hope all will go well with her. I ought to get letters from you again in a day or two of the 1st June, but mine have to go to Peshawur. The papers came in to-day. You had just received the telegraphic news of the 3rd Cavalry having mutinied at Meerut on the 10th May. Lord Ellenburgh made a good speech, altho' he did not actually pitch on the real cause. The fact is, no one knows what it is. A combination of affairs I believe, but the Musalmans[1] are at the bottom of it. Good-night, my own Mother. I will write a line or two before Post time to-morrow.

July 25th.—A nice wet day again, which has as much effect in keeping the Pandies quiet as anything else. The Doctor told me this morning that my wound had taken the turn and would now heal, so I hope to be off the sick list in 10 days or a fortnight. Good-bye dearest Mother. Give my kind love to the General, Harrie, Innes, John, Hamilton and all, and ever believe me, my own Mother, your fond and affec. son,

FRED. ROBERTS.

Tell Harrie to write to Maggie Boisragon. She has been so good to me and sent me all sorts of little comforts all the way from Lahore.

[1] *Musalman*, a believer, a Mahomedan; from the Persian *Moslem*, belief.

CAMP BEFORE DELHI,
Aug. 12th and 13th, 1857.

MY DEAREST FATHER—I have written to my Mother or Harriet every Mail since I came here, giving a slight account of how affairs are going on, and in my last I think I mentioned something about dating this letter from the "King's Palace," instead of "before Delhi," but we are still at the old work, holding our own quietly, and giving the Pandies a thrashing whenever they venture too close. You will see from the enclosed state of the Troops that, altho' nominally we have several Regiments here, in actual numbers we have but few. At no period I imagine have the European Regiments, both Queen's and Company's, been so weak, with the exception of the 8th and 61st, the others are all *whole* Regiments, a few men only being left behind at their respective Depots, and yet not one comes up to the strength of a healthy Wing. On the 8th June, when we first arrived here, I believe, by an assault, we could probably have taken possession of the City, the enemy never doubting but that they would easily beat us off, contented themselves by taking up a very strong position, some 3 miles in advance of the Cantonments, with a strong reserve to fall back upon, in and about the Cantonments themselves, and as we have since ascertained, did little towards strengthening the Batteries on the City Walls, besides which, their numbers then did not probably exceed 16, or 17,000 fighting men. Had we, however, taken the City our Force was, at that time, so small that we would have had great difficulty in merely keeping it without being able to render assistance to any other part of the country. Neither have we been able to do that *directly*, from our present Camp, but the mere fact of our being here in front of Delhi has attracted all the mutineers to this one spot, without which loadstone, they would certainly have wandered all over the country. Our communication with the Punjab would have been cut off by their getting round to the rear. We should have had the greatest possible difficulty in getting supplies, as with the numbers their Army has swelled to, they could have surrounded the whole City and rendered our foraging a work of great danger, instead of which we have had a daily post in from the North West, and after the first few days supplies of every description have been plentiful. Besides this, had a report been spread that the Mutineers were on their way to Umballa and the Punjab, the people would have risen universally with them, even now it is generally believed that the Putiala Rajah,[1]

[1] "The Maharaja of Patiala and the other Phulkian Chiefs remained perfectly loyal, and performed the important service of keeping open communications between Delhi and the Punjab" (*Forty-One Years in India*).

This sketch is a very rough one, but pretty accurate. – our guns are as you will see on the ridge of the hill chiefly – Hindoo Rao's House being the strong support – where the Goorkhas have been from the commencement! Nothing will induce them to leave. Since the 14th July – the last day we had hard fighting in the Subzee Mundee – the Walls, old houses &c. have been pretty levelled – so that the Pandies don't like coming there. – Our attack when we do go, will be on the Cashmere and Moree Bastion. – J.R.

Detail of the Army before Delhi from June 8th – August 10th 1857

		Present for duty on 10th August 1857					Sick & Wounded on 10th August 1857					Killed & Wounded up to 10th August 1857							Total on service from 8th June to 10th August 1857			Arrived before Delhi
		Officers	Men	Native Officers	Natives	Horses	Officers	Men	Native Officers	Natives	Horses	Officers killed	Officers wounded	Men killed	Men wounded	Natives killed	Natives wounded	Horses killed & wounded	Officers	Men	Natives	
	Staff	39	598	-	-	323	11	81	-	-	52	2	19	26	107	-	-	117	52	705	·	8th June – in part.
x	Artillery	30	·	-	-	-	4	-	-	-	-	3	4	·	-	-	-	-	33	·	·	do. do.
xx	Engineers	26	39	-	-	-	2	9	-	-	-	2	4	4	-	-	-	-	30	52	·	do. do.
	Cavalry	18	570	-	-	520	7	49	-	-	43	3	-	31	36	-	-	75	28	640	-	do.
1st Brigade	75th Queens	16	502	-	-	-	1	101	-	-	-	3	8	36	93	-	-	-	20	639	-	do.
1st Brigade	1st Fusiliers	17	487	-	-	-	4	122	-	-	-	-	5	30	150	-	-	-	21	639	-	do
1st Brigade	Kumaon Bat.	4	-	13	435	-	1	-	-	27	-	1	1	-	-	2	-	-	6	477	-	1st August –
2nd Brigade	60th Rifles	15	251	-	-	-	6	88	-	-	-	3	10	44	145	-	-	-	24	375	-	8th June.
2nd Brigade	2nd Fusiliers	20	493	-	-	-	4	138	-	-	-	2	4	21	94	-	-	-	26	652	-	do.
2nd Brigade	Sirmoor Bat.	4	-	9	319	-	2	-	2	95	-	1	4	-	-	43	191	-	7	468	-	do.
3rd Brigade	8th Queens	15	153	-	-	-	2	106	-	-	-	1	3	17	25	-	-	-	18	276	-	23rd June
3rd Brigade	61st Queens	12	249	-	-	-	4	110	-	-	-	-	4	3	21	-	-	-	16	362	-	do
3rd Brigade	4th Sikhs	4	-	4	365	-	3	-	4	65	-	1	2	-	-	16	37	-	8	450	-	do
	Guide Corps	4	-	4	196	-	2	-	3	55	-	1	7	-	-	40	156	-	7	298	-	12th June.
	Coke's Corps	5	-	16	709	-	1	-	3	47	-	2	1	-	-	16	74	-	8	788		1st July.
		229	3342	46	2024	1343	54	804	12	289	95	25	76	218	671	117	458	192				

x. 18-9PR. H.A. GUNS. 12-9PR. H.A. GUNS. besides heavy ARTILLERY

xx ARTILLERY, ENGINEERS & CAVALRY have some natives attached, chiefly Irregulars, newly raised –

Besides these Casualties several Officers & men have died of disease &c. or gone away for change of air.

[illegible] Horse Artillery, D.A. [illegible] of the Army.

as well as several Sirdars in the Jullundur, and other Doabs[1] of the Punjab are greatly inclined to join the rebels, but seeing all work and business carried on as usual, they have sense enough to feel that our Government is not quite at an end, although there is no doubt it has received a great shock. Our position here is certainly, *by Nature*, a wonderfully secure one, and if the "Pandies" could not have found a better place than Delhi as the Headquarters of their Mutiny, with an unlimited Magazine at their disposal, I doubt if we could have been so well off anywhere. Providence has assisted us in every way. From the very beginning, the weather has been most propitious, and in Cantonments I have never seen Troops so healthy as they are here now. Cholera occasionally pays us a visit, but that must always be expected in a large standing Camp. The River completely protects our left front and flank, while the large Jheel[2] which runs away to the S.W. is at this season quite impassable for miles, and prevents any surprise on our right flank, so that a few Cavalry are sufficient as a guard for 3 faces of our position, and we are consequently enabled to devote our

[1] *Doab*, a tract of land lying between two rivers which finally unite; from the Persian, *do*, two; and *ab*, water.

[2] *Jheel* or *jhil*, a Hindi word signifying a marsh, a morass.

whole Force to keep our Front from surprise, but to do this whenever we are attacked in any force takes almost every available man in camp. At a moderate calculation the enemy must muster now nearly 40,000 men, besides guns unlimited, and they certainly work them well. Their Infantry also fight well, but the Cavalry, both regular and irregular, are not worth one sixpence. They do nothing but run away. I always thought I would like to be a Cavalry Officer, but I have seen enough to convince me that they are all show, as far as regards actual fighting. At a siege, or whatever this may be called, they have not many opportunities, but on the few occasions I have seen them out, they have always disappointed me, European as well as Native, not half the dash they ought to have. I can't understand the reason. Officers I know personally to be fine plucky fellows, have lost splendid chances of a good charge from merely hesitating, and I begin to think it requires a smarter fellow to be a good cavalry leader than in any other arm.[1] I would far prefer the Infantry to Cavalry, but *the* service is no doubt the *Artillery*! whether up in the Batteries with the heavy guns or in

[1] "Officers should possess all the qualities of good sportsmen. They should be fine riders, have a keen eye for country, and be thoroughly well educated" (Introduction by Lord Roberts to *War and the Arme Blanche*, by Erskine Childers, 1910).

the open with the light ones, you are sure to see most of the fun, and I never met such brave plucky fellows as our gunners, nothing alarms, nothing disconcerts them, and then you have the satisfaction of knowing that all are looking to the Artillery, foes as well as friends respect it. Altho' you used so often to advise, my dear old Father, my working hard and getting into the Engineers while at Addiscombe, instead of leading the idle, careless life I used to there, I can assure you that, had I the offer, I would not change for anything. In a Station and during times of peace our Engineers lead a life I should detest, building barracks and keeping accounts, and, on service, I far prefer Artillery work, not but that at times our Engineers are perhaps exposed to greater danger. They do their business well, whatever it is, and a finer Corps there cannot be, but let me be a "*Gunner*"!! Of all the Infantry Regiments here, the most distinguished is the 60th Rifles.[1] They and the gallant little Goorkhas in the Sirmoor Battalion[2] have borne the brunt of the whole affair and suffered fearfully. After them comes your old Regiment, the 1st Fusiliers, and the Guides. This morning we

[1] The writer, in later years, was wont to say that his admiration for the 60th Rifles before Delhi inspired him with a wish that he might one day have a son in the Regiment. A wish that was fulfilled.

[2] Now the 2nd King Edward's Own Gurkhas.

surprised a Battery they had recently erected rather too near to our Piquets, and in such a position that our heavy guns could not bear on it, so it was decided to carry it by assault. The 1st Fusiliers and Coke's Punjab Rifles (also a fine Corps) did the business well, each Regiment capturing two guns. We always suffer immensely in Officers. You will see by my return that a third of our number have been killed or wounded in the two months, besides which Cholera has carried off several. However, we shall soon bring this business to an end. To-morrow a reinforcement under Nicholson comes in, consisting of 1000 European Infantry and about the same number of natives, and a 2nd Class Siege Train has left Ferozepore *en route* to this. Whether Grant[1] arrives or not, as soon as the train comes, we shall, I hope, go in. Having waited so long, it is better perhaps to finish up well by shelling the town for several days, and making a decent breach. All agree taking it by assault is out of the question, and our Batteries, on account of the great height of the glacis will have to be advanced so close that a practicable breach will be made in a day or two, after we once

[1] On the death of General Anson, General, afterwards Field-Marshal, Sir Patrick Grant, commanding in Madras, was appointed Commander-in-Chief in Bengal, pending the arrival of General Sir Colin Campbell from England.

commence, so there will be no delay when once we have the train. I do long so to see the inside of this hateful place. It has been proved beyond a doubt that the King's son shot several European men and women with his own hand. Yet, even with this, there are some people who talk of a pardon for the "*poor misguided King and his family*." I only trust all the women and children will have been removed, for once inside, few will be spared. It will be an extraordinary day for those that see the end of it, if the Pandies only wait to fight, but I sometimes think the greater part will be off with the plunder they have got, and we shall then have to follow them up somewhere else. Sir H. Lawrence[1] will be a sad loss if the report of his death is really true. Almost every one here has lost some dear friend or relation by the hands of the villains, which is enough to make us eager for revenge, not only on account of the death they have suffered, but to try and wipe out some of the injuries that were heaped on them both while they were alive and after-

[1] The Chief Commissioner of Oude; he was mortally wounded by a shell during the siege of Lucknow. The measures taken by Sir Henry Lawrence on the outbreak of the Mutiny he had predicted fourteen years before were in marked contrast to the indecision displayed in some quarters; by his sagacity and forethought he made it possible for his fellow-countrymen to weather the storm from July to November, and his knowledge of, and influence over, the native soldiers kept them loyal—a matter of the utmost importance, for without their aid the glorious defence of the Residency could not have been maintained.

wards. The first day our troops arrived here, they found a cart-load of dead men and women, all naked, between the Cantonments and City Walls, who had evidently been there from the first day of the massacre. I have given you this long account of our numerical strength, position, etc., as I have no doubt there will be plenty of people in England, as there are on all these occasions, who will be ready to abuse all that has been done here. Even in this Country, several cry out to take Delhi, without any more delay, as if we were not one and all anxious to do so, but the fate of all India depends on our success. Were a failure to be the result, God only knows what would take place. The whole country would, I really believe, turn against us. You, who know Delhi so well and can understand what troops we really have, will be able to judge as to whether our policy has been the correct one. I have taken great care to give you the returns properly, so you need not fear about showing them to any one. We have received only one *direct* communication from Genl. Havelock as yet, dated 26th July, on the River, near Cawnpore, in which he stated that he was on his way to Lucknow, so that we can only form surmises as to his present whereabouts, but I do not expect to see his force here before the 5th or

6th prox.[1] However, I still hope to date my next letter from the Palace! My wound has not healed up yet. I had no idea it would have taken a month. The Doctors say from being so near the spine, it is delayed. What bothers me most is, I can't ride. However, I am very jolly and happy, and appreciate my luck and feel thankful to God when I see so many poor fellows around me infinitely worse off. Harriet's dear letter of the 17th June I received a few days ago. You were then on the point of starting for Scotland, after which, Harriet said, that you were going to Buxton to try another month of Water cure. I trust most sincerely that you will be benefited by the change, and that you may all return to Suir View[2] well and hearty. I feel so happy that you are all at home, out of this country. I expect to read all sorts of rubbish in the papers about paucity of Officers with Native Regiments, and not sufficiently mixing with their men. Why, the only Corps we have here are Irregular ones who never have more than 3 Officers! The Lumsdens[3] are still in Candahar. I wish

[1] During the earlier period of the siege it was confidently expected that the force before Delhi would be reinforced by troops sent up country from Calcutta and other places. Later allusions to "help from below" refer to this.

[2] A house on the banks of the Suir near Waterford.

[3] The brothers, Harry and Peter Lumsden (afterwards General Sir Harry Lumsden, K.C.S.I., and General Sir Peter Lumsden, G.C.B.), had been sent on a mission to Kandahar.

I could see them out of it. Hyder Khan treats them very civilly, but as Peter writes to me, "we are a kind of gentlemanly prisoners." Of all the Dost's[1] sons, Hyder is the only one, I believe, who is favourable to us, the others are endeavouring to work him up to an attack on Peshawur now that they hear we are in this "fix." The Dost himself is too wise an old man, but should he die the sons will kick up a row to a certainty, and then the poor Lumsdens will not be in an enviable position. However, ere many months we will have such a force of Europeans in the Country that I hope all these petty Rajahs will rise, so that we may make one sweep, and wind up by taking *Cashmere*! where I shall be very happy to spend every hot weather roaming about the beautiful places there. I half expect to see Hamilton's and George's name in the Papers as "coming out," when the next Mail arrives, yet, unless they are well, I hope they will remain at home, for all the fun will be over before they can be here. Dear Hamilton. I would give a great deal to have him in Camp sometimes. His Regiment is close alongside of my tent, or perhaps "my tent is close alongside of his Regiment" would be the proper way?! Were I in George's

[1] Dost Mahomed Khan, Amir of Kabul. In *Forty-One Years* Lord Roberts tells of the part played by the Dost in keeping Afghanistan aloof during the troublous months of the Mutiny.

place, I should be inclined to leave my wife behind until things got more settled. He will probably have to join a column marching about the country. Even if he gets to a station, there is scarcely one below Umballa habitable.

13*th*.—This is the last safe day, and as my letter has already become a volume, I will bring it to an end. Is there any chance of Pat Grant being made C. in Chief?[1] This business has been strangely fatal to our Chiefs. The 5 men who formed the "Council of War" first in Umballa are all dead. Genl. Anson and Barnard, Brigadier Hallifax and Colonel Mowatt—of cholera—and Colonel Chester killed in action. Then came Genl. Reed, who had to leave half dead, and Chamberlain as Adjutant-General, whose wound will incapacitate him from work for months. Our present Commander, Wilson, of the Artillery, is pretty tough and I hope he may have better luck. We are generally attacked on our right front, but when the enemy come in force, it employs every man in camp. The Pandies can afford reliefs, which we cannot, and on some occasions our men have been on the *qui vive* for 60 hours at a time. All do their work cheerfully, and no

[1] See note, p. 36.

Army could, I am sure, do more than this has. Good-bye. Give my best love to dearest Mother and Harriet.—Believe me, ever your affect. son,

FRED. ROBERTS.

Tell Mother or "Harrie" to write to me every Mail, and tell me how you are all getting on.—F. R. God Bless you all.—F. R.

. . . . . .

This sketch is a very rough one, but pretty accurate. Our defences are, as you will see, on the ridge of the Hill chiefly, Hindoo Rao's House being the strong support, where the Goorkhas have been from the commencement! Nothing will induce them to leave. Since the 14th July, the last day we had hard fighting in the Subjhee Mundee, the Walls, old houses, etc., have been greatly levelled, so that the Pandies don't like coming there. Our *attack, when we* DO GO, will be on the Cashmere and Moree Bastion.

F. R.

CAMP BEFORE DELHI,
Aug. 25th, 1857.

MY DEAREST HARRIET—I had hoped that to-day's post would have brought me a letter from some of you, as the Mail of the 10th July has arrived, but I fancy that my letters are

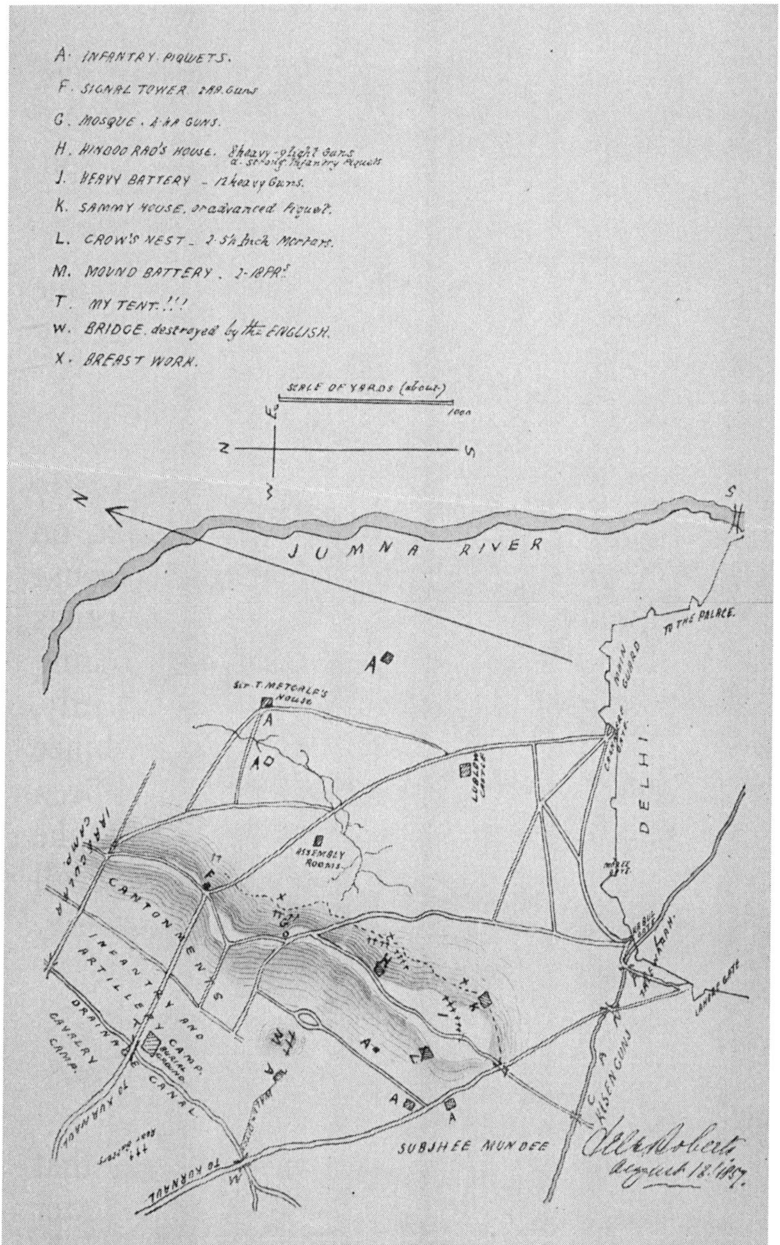
A. INFANTRY PIQUETS.
F. SIGNAL TOWER 2 18 Guns
G. MOSQUE. 2 18 GUNS.
H. HINDOO RAO'S HOUSE. 5 heavy - 9 light Guns
a Strong Infantry Piquets
J. HEAVY BATTERY - 12 heavy Guns.
K. SAMMY HOUSE. or advanced Piquet.
L. CROW'S NEST - 2 5½ Inch Mortars.
M. MOUND BATTERY. 2 - 18 PR.S
T. MY TENT !!!
W. BRIDGE destroyed by the ENGLISH.
X. BREAST WORK.
SCALE OF YARDS (about)
1000
N
S
E
W
JUMNA RIVER
TO THE PALACE.
MAIN GUARD
Sir T. METCALFE'S HOUSE
LUDLOW CASTLE
DELHI
ASSEMBLY ROOMS
CANTONMENTS
INFANTRY AND ARTILLERY CAMP.
CAVALRY CAMP.
DRAINAGE CANAL
BURIAL GROUND
TO KURNAUL
SUBJHEE MUNDEE
LAHORE GATE
August 18. 1857.

delayed at Lahore and that I shall not hear until to-morrow, when I trust to get a dear long letter from old England. How glad you must all be that Hamilton and nearly all of the *long* family are at home, and not out in this horrid country during these never-to-be-forgotten disasters and massacres. I wish most sincerely that every woman and child were well away, and that these fiendish Sepoys had met with men only on whom their cruelties might have been practised without causing that feeling of intense horror which must pervade every one when they read what our poor unfortunate women and helpless children have had to undergo. A day or two ago we received an account of the tragedy at Cawnpore from a Lieut. Delafosse, one out of 4 who survived. I would send you a copy of it, but it would only make you sad. It is quite bad enough hearing in a general way, without the details from each separate station. A few things I can tell you. As soon as the Regiments mutinied on the 2nd or 3rd June, the whole of the European inhabitants collected near one of the Barracks and entrenched themselves as well as they could. However, the ruffians in a day or two set fire to the thatch, and women, children, sick and wounded from the 12th June to the 27th June, had no shelter or covering, not only exposed to the climate, a June in India!! (we all in tents were nearly roasted), but night and day the enemy fired round shot, shell and musketry at them. Was there ever anything so fearful? Several died from Cholera, Fever, etc., and the remainder, after being promised their lives if they gave up all the treasure they had, surrendered and were taken down to boats which these blackguards promised should convey them to Allahabad. They were no sooner in the boats than Artillery commenced firing on them, and ere they could get the boats under weigh, the Infantry and Cavalry surrounded them. What happened after this Delafosse did not know, beyond the fate of those who were in the same boat with him. For 2 days and nights they floated down the river, being fired at the whole way, and at last stuck on a sandbank. Fourteen of them then determined to charge the enemy which they did, and 5 only got back to the river, about a mile below where the boat was stranded. These 5 jumped into the river and 4 of them succeeded in getting away, swimming for some 6 miles, when they were hailed from the shore by villagers, who took them in and gave them shelter for a month, until our troops passed by. The rest are all supposed to have been killed, whether at that time, or the day before our troops reached Cawnpore is at present doubtful, but the general idea seems to be that the men were all killed on the 27th June and the women kept by these fellows until they heard Europeans were close by, and then they were all murdered. Poor little Harry Warde was at Cawnpore. His name is on the list, but no remark opposite to it, so he probably was murdered at the last. Col. and Mrs. Lindsay (Lillie Don that was) died of fever, but I enclose you a list of all that were there, as far as Delafosse could recollect. Those with fever, etc., opposite to their names died before the 27th June, but besides this sad long list, there were many others who had come in from smaller stations for refuge, and whose names were not known, but God only knows how many merchants, shopkeepers, pensioners, etc. Nothing has ever happened in the world like this, and I hope such a fearful tragedy may never come again. It makes one very melancholy hearing day after day of some old friend being no more, and in my mind has excited such a feeling of horror that I would undergo cheerfully any privation, any amount of work, living in the hopes of a *revenge* on these cruel murderers. This feeling is shared by every European in the Camp. All long to be at Delhi, and it is this alone I really believe that has supported and kept up our gallant soldiers. I could not have imagined any men could have worked as they have done, from Officers and all you never hear a grumble. Our Rifles and Gunners are beyond all praise. There are so few of them that they almost live in the trenches and Batteries, and have had their numbers sadly thinned. However, I think now that our days *outside* Delhi are really numbered. About the 1st prox. a siege train, 200 Rifles and 100 Artillery men will arrive, the last of our reinforcements. Help from below[1] is out of the question now. Lucknow has not been relieved yet, so we must do for ourselves, and right well we will do it. From the nature of the ground (all stones) it is impossible to make regular approaches, so we must trust to having a dark night and erect our Batteries, some 500 yards nearer the City Walls than they now are. Once in position, we will soon destroy the upper defences, and make a kind of a breach, but the wall is so well covered by the glacis that the breach cannot be a very first-rate one. However, we'll get in to a certainty, and once hold of their ramparts will teach our friends a lesson. I calculate the 10th September will see us inside—delay will ruin us. Our men are even now getting very sickly. Cholera keeps paying us visits and every day we

[1] See note, p. 39.

shall get worse instead of better. I am going to turn gunner again when our new Batteries are up. From one thing and another Artillery Officers have diminished greatly, so Johnson,[1] the Assistant-Adjutant-General, and Fred. Roberts, the Assistant-Quartermaster-General of Artillery, are to have a Battery between them, and work away until the City falls, when we go back to our old duties. I am now quite well and come off the sick list to-day. Six weeks since I was wounded. I had no idea at first it would have taken so long, but the hole was deeper than I knew of, and being near the spine did not heal so quickly as it otherwise would have. Jemmy Lind arrived in Camp the other day, in command of some Irregular Horse. He is a fine fellow and will distinguish himself if he has a chance. He was ordered out this morning with a Force, and has left a letter for his sister with me to post. In case, however, of its not reaching, you might write, dearest Harriet, when you receive this and tell them he is quite well and as jolly as possible. Caroline Hay's brother is here. He is the image of his mother and equally mad. In the recent rows his wigs were all stolen, and as he has no, nor ever had, I believe, any, hair, he cuts a most comical figure. I have never spoken

[1] Afterwards General Sir Edwin Johnson, G.C.B.

to him, but will do so some day. ——, who married —— ——, is also here. He is, I am sorry to say, *a drunken young snob*, and to my great regret, told me the other day that one of his wife's little sisters had come out to him. It is perfectly impossible he can support her. From the little I have seen of him here, I should say his pay would scarcely cover his monthly Mess bills. Poor little ——. They say she is such a nice girl and doats on this blockhead. It would be almost a mercy were he killed here, for he will most certainly have to leave the Army some day, unless he changes, and that I should say he is not likely to do. I hope to hear that your trip to Scotland has done both you and mother a great deal of good. It is a great nuisance making a start from home, but a change is always beneficial, and you ought to go away at least once a year. Hamilton's name is not among the list of passengers, so I hope the Doctors have recommended his remaining some time longer in England. Lord Ellenborough talks great nonsense about stopping the Canal water. Why, Delhi is on the very edge of the "Jumna." He must know this surely. The rest of his speech of the 29th June is very good, and shows that he sees farther than most. It is difficult to say what the result of all this will be, but I fancy John

Company is at an end. Good-bye, dearest Harriet. Write to me every Mail *long, long letters.* Give my fondest love to the General and my Mother, and accept the same, my own darling sister.—From your ever affect. brother,

FRED. ROBERTS.

Do you think the enclosed likeness looks *less* savage?

Give my love to dear Innes, Sherston and Hamilton, if with you, and tell the latter I will write to him from the Palace of Delhi.—F. R. I have not copied out the list after all. It is too fearful.

CAMP BEFORE DELHI,
August 28th, 1857.

MY OWN DEAREST MOTHER—A notice has just come round to say that an Express dâk starts this afternoon to overtake the Overland Mail, so I must write you a few lines, altho' I sent Harriet a long letter the other day, for I am sure you will be anxious to hear how I am getting on. I also want to tell you not to direct my letters as usual, to Peshawur, but to "Lahore." If I return to the former place, I can always have them forwarded, and, if not, I shall get them nearly a week sooner than I do now. Nothing has come for me yet of the 10th July Mail, because the blockhead at Lahore will send my letters to Peshawur instead of to this direct, although I have written and begged him not to. My wound has completely healed up. I am off the sick list and as jolly as possible. Looking forward most anxiously to see the inside of Delhi. We had a great victory a day or two ago. A large force of the enemy left the City and started in the direction of our rear, evidently intending to cut off the siege train. Nicholson was sent out, gave them a thrashing and captured 11 guns. I was told off to go as Quartermaster-General to the party, but Nicholson said, much as he would like to have me, he would not consent to my accompanying him, as he felt sure I was not strong enough just now for hard work. I was sadly disappointed, but immediately on his return, he came to see me and spoke so kindly and said he wanted me to be well for the grand business, and that I might rely on his never leaving me behind, that I felt quite happy again. Nicholson is really the only Commander we have here, now that Chamberlain is laid up, and, in my opinion, he is superior to him. Such a sensible fellow, a man in every sense of the word. He is very kind to me, and, as you see, Mother dear, a true friend to me. I made out a map for him of the country he would have to go over, without which, he said, he would never have gained his victory, as no one with him knew the road. A precious conceited fellow am I not, Mother, telling you all these stories of myself. I hope long ere this troops are coming out from England in large numbers. The Army of Bengal cannot do much more damage, but Bombay will, I feel sure, follow the example, and Madras probably also, unless they see it would be useless, from the force of Europeans that ought to come out at once. The Court of Directors seem to be doing their best to be kicked out, making speeches and abusing their Officers. Were they to blame, it was surely their business to have taken care that a new system was introduced, and not allowed such men to remain in the Army. They are trying a nasty, cowardly dodge which will ruin themselves. The Officers are not to blame. The whole Mutiny from beginning to end is almost unaccountable, but if any one is to blame, it is the Indian Government, made up of men who have never been out of Calcutta in all their lives and who know positively nothing of Native soldiers. Our Officers have had only too much faith and confidence in their men, and many a gallant fellow has gone to his last home from this feeling, almost amounting to infatuation. However, our first business is to get out of the scrape, and find out the cause afterwards, and the sooner we take Delhi the better. I don't believe myself there is one single Native in the whole country who would not go against us, if they did not think they were better off by remaining on our side. All our levies find, Rupees and plunder, is to be had from dead Sepoys, and imagining they are too late in the field themselves to get it from us, they prefer taking it from "Pandies" to getting none, and consequently stand by us; but delay will ruin us. Several fellows have been convicted of treachery, and amongst them, a few days ago, some of the Artillery Natives attached to the Magazine. We are obliged to employ them for want of Europeans, but as for their remaining loyal is out of the question and the damage they could do us is fearful to think of. Of course, every precaution is taken, and I think all are convinced that we must go at Delhi by the 9th or 10th prox. at any risks. Write to me every Mail, my own Mother, long letters. If you only knew the pleasure it is to me out here getting your dear letters. God Bless you all. With my fondest love.—Ever your fond and affect. son,

FRED. ROBERTS.

CAMP BEFORE DELHI,
Sept. 7th, 1857.

MY DEAREST MOTHER—I believe I am in full time for the Mail, but as I go into the Batteries to-morrow, and will probably not have a chance of writing to you for some days, I must send you a few lines before I go to sleep this evening. I received to-day the General's and Harriet's letters of the 23rd July. I can't tell you what pleasure it afforded me to hear that you were all well, and if you could only have told me of dear Innes getting through her troubles safely, I should have been quite happy. However, I hope you will be able to do so in your next. I don't write to her for I have not very much time to spare, but I know you will send her my letters to read. I wish Hamilton could have remained at home with you, darling Mother, during the present crisis. It is sad indeed for you having both your sons in this horrid country. Yet, ere Hamilton can arrive, I trust most sincerely all will be over. Our work here is nearly done. The 1st[1] Battery is getting into position now while I am writing, and to-morrow night the 2nd will be made. This is *the* Battery, in advance of all others and to make the principal

[1] The sites of the breaching batteries are marked and can still be identified.

breach—it is manned by the "pets," *i.e.* all Staff Officers,—and short work we will make of it. Once in there, we have to remain until the time of the assault, as the approaches are none of the best—without Sappers it is hard work getting on at all, but every one bears a hand willingly and on the morning of the 12th *at the latest*, Delhi will, with God's help, be ours. The City was taken by us the first time on the 11th Sept., 1803. We may perhaps manage to come to time in '57, but I give it till the 12th. Once we are in a Column starts in pursuit, and with this I am going as Quartermaster-General!! Am I not lucky, Mother dear, altho' only officiating, I am sent before the others in the same Department. I fancy we shall make first of all for Agra, and then bend our steps to Central India or Oude. As the Pandies may show fight, the latter place appears to me the most likely. Lucknow, according to the letters we received to-day dated 27th ult. was still besieged, and as the majority of the Mutineers come from that part, they will probably hasten to join their friends there, in the hope of being able to murder some more helpless women and children. However, we give no quarter, every single man we find is killed, so perhaps, after all, if the rascals will only fight, many may not survive to tell the tale.

My own Mother, I wish I could see you once again. I do not anticipate any great struggle, yet some lives must be sacrificed, and it may please God to take mine. I am ready and willing to give it. No one ever died in a better cause, but I feel as if all would go well. I never remember being in better spirits or so thoroughly jolly. After the long, weary time we have spent here at the very worst season of the year, the mere idea of a change makes all feel happy. I can scarcely realise that this is the last night I have to spend in my tent before these horrid Walls, the next 2 or 3 in the Batteries and then I hope many miles beyond, following up and punishing these fiends, wherever we may meet them. What fun it will be seeing dear Hamilton again. His Regiment is, I think, almost certain to be in the pursuing Column, so I shall probably come across him by the end of next month. I am in just the appointment he would like, if he is as fond of riding as I am. The whole day has sometimes to be spent in the saddle, but nothing I enjoy more, particularly in the cold weather. It is still hot here, however, and I anticipate one or two days' grilling in the trenches. Once Delhi falls, the reaction will be felt all over the country. One-third of our force can be spared to go on, one-third to remain here, and what will be of more service than anything else, one-third to march back to the Punjab. It will restore confidence to the wavering and make those who have hitherto remained true to us feel that they have done wisely. All Natives are the same, and I believe we are as thoroughly hated in the Punjab as elsewhere; but then their overthrow has been recent, and instead of being ruled over by idiot after idiot, as in our older Provinces, they have had the very best men in the country. If the same policy is pursued, and our Army is composed of Sikhs and Punjabees, the opposite extreme, we shall have the same work again some day. Without being severe, I have always kept my servants well in order, once they trip, I give it them well. Yet, all this time, when whole sets have gone off and many Officers are without one, I have only lost a syce and he must have been murdered, as he left all his traps behind him and I really believe that my fellows will accompany me anywhere. One regret I shall feel, Mother, in leaving this place is the thoughts of so many gallant fellows whose bodies will remain here for ever. I don't know how many friends I have lost. Poor Yorke was the first. After his death a new half of the burial ground was commenced on, and that is now very nearly filled—in two short months.

My old chum Lambert of the 1st Fusiliers is still to the fore, and as nice a fellow as ever, yet, strange to say, he is not a great favourite in his Regiment. I can't make it out, for he has every manly quality. Tell Harrie to remember me kindly to all the Wardes[1] when she writes. I never was so fond of a family, from the old Admiral down to little Sonie. Poor Harry, I am afraid, has been murdered at Cawnpore. Out of the whole station, only some 4 or 5 have escaped, and his name has never been mentioned as one. Should I go to Cawnpore, I will make every enquiry, and try and find out the poor lad's fate. I should like to see George out here, but if he is still suffering he had better remain at home, as we shall, no doubt, be unsettled and knocked about all over the country for some time to come. Well, now, Mother, I must go to bed, as it is the last quiet night I shall have probably for the next week or so. God Bless you all. With my best love to the dear old General, Harrie and all.—Ever believe me, my fondly loved Mother, your very affect. son,

FRED. ROBERTS.

If I possibly can, I will write you from INSIDE Delhi. Should I not be able to, I will

[1] Of Squerries Court, Westerham.

ask Maggie Boisragon to do so from Lahore. She will hear by telegraph how all goes, and her letter should be in time for the Mail. Write to me, Mother dearest, *every Mail long letters*, and direct "*Lahore*."

CAMP "DELHI,"
Sept. 16*th*, 1857.

MY DEAREST MOTHER—At last we are inside this wretched City, and altho' we have not reduced the whole place, have got such a hold that no amount of Pandies will drive us out. On the morning of the 14th we stormed in 3 Columns for 4 days before which I had been in the Breaching Battery working day and night at the heavy guns. We made a clipping breach, and our men got up famously. Until we were inside the walls, our loss was very slight, but moving up through various streets, we lost fearfully, some 40 or 50 officers and about 800 men. I escaped thro' God's blessing, but in the evening, in a small scrimmage in which Norman,[1] Johnson, Assistant-Adjutant-General of Artillery, and I, were engaged, I had my horse shot and a slight crack near the hip. However, my horse I did not value much, and by and bye will get compensation

[1] Afterwards Field-Marshal Sir Henry Norman, G.C.B., G.C.M.G.

for it. The first day all was confusion. Soldiers lost their Regiments in the streets, and I half expected we should be attacked during the night. We were not, and altho' I had nothing but the ground and my saddle to rest on, I slept so soundly. For 5 days I had never been quiet, and what with the noise of our guns in the battery (9-24 PRs.) the sun, etc., etc., I was very nearly done for. Mother, you would scarcely know me. My face and hands are as black as a coal from exposure, but I am in most capital health and as jolly as possible. I am now with the Headquarters again, and we are all living at Skinner's house, just inside the City. Securing the whole place will be a work of time, as we can only occupy street after street gradually. This morning we took the Magazine and only had 3 men wounded. These cowardly rascals never stay when they hear a cheer. Such a scene of desolation as the whole place is—the Church is a ruin, and all the European houses, and our men now sack and destroy all the Native ones. Ladies' bonnets, flowers, all sorts of things you find, these blackguards had stolen. Yesterday, upon one of the Batteries, I found a portmanteau with "Miss Jennings" on it. Her Father was the Clergyman here. She was an extremely pretty girl, and was murdered coming out of

Church on the 11th May.[1] I was just in time this morning to save the lives of 2 poor Native women. They were both wounded and had concealed themselves in a little house. Another hour, and both, I believe, would have died from exhaustion; when I gave them some water they were so grateful, for they seemed to expect I should kill them. General Nicholson is, I am afraid, mortally wounded. He led his Column like no other man could, and in him we lose our best Officer. The Engineers and 1st Fusiliers had each 9 or 10 Officers knocked over. The Artillery only had 2, but we suffered severely during the time we were breaching. However, our work is not over yet, Mother. It will take at least a week to clear the City, and many more fine fellows will be sacrificed. I hope this will be in time for the Mail, tho' I scarcely expect it. However, you will be glad to receive it whenever it reaches. Once we hold Delhi the road to Cawnpore will soon be opened, and the Sepoys driven out of their stronghold will dwindle away. Hay is badly wounded, shot thro' the mouth. I fear he has a poor chance of recovering, as they can't feed him. I have no time for a long letter, so must say good-bye, Mother dearest. Give my kind love

[1] Miss Jennings and her father were among the people murdered in the Fort.

to the General and Harrie and send this to dear Innes to read. Love to her and John.—Ever your fondly attached son,

FRED. ROBERTS.

CAMP DADREE,
Sept. 26th, 1857.

MY DEAREST FATHER—I daresay you will like to hear of the assault and subsequent capture of Delhi, and of our movements since, and as I am now on my way to disturbed districts, where dâks cannot be very regular, I'll send you a few lines to-day. On the 14th, we assaulted. Two breaches were made, up which 2 Columns mounted, 1 Column went thro' the Cashmere Gate, which was blown open with Powder bags, and the 4th Column attacked the suburbs. Since war was ever known, I fancy no assault took place as ours did. For fear of losing the men in the streets, it was decided not to attack until the day was sufficiently advanced for us to see clearly, and what with one delay and another, it was sunrise ere we reached the breach.[1] Up our men went

[1] "Many of the men belonging to the regiments of the storming force had been on picquet all night, and it took some time for them to rejoin their respective corps. A further delay was caused by our having to destroy the partial repairs to the breaches which the enemy had succeeded in effecting during the night, notwithstanding the heavy fire we kept up (*Forty-One Years in India*).

beautifully like a pack of hounds. We gunners had done our work so well that the Breach was perfect, and we gained the ramparts with a comparatively slight loss. Blowing in the gate was a work of great danger. In addition to heavy firing from the loopholed walls, the rebels had actually the wicket of the gate open all the time our Engineers were fixing and firing the bags, and, of course, great slaughter ensued. One after another of the Sappers held the Portfire and were knocked over before they could succeed in lighting the hose. At last they went with a crash, and now our Columns were all inside. From this time, we suffered severely. Two Columns followed the road under the ramparts occupying the Bastions up to the Cabul Gate, where one halted while the other pushed on under that magnificent fellow Nicholson. It consisted of the 75th Queen's, your old Regiment, the 1st Fusiliers and some Sikhs, about 1000 men (the strength of all our Columns). They went on for some distance, but near the Lahore Gate, the road became so narrow that only 2 men could go abreast, and down this heavy guns were playing with grape, besides heavy musketry from the neighbouring houses. Down went the men. At the head poor Nicholson fell mortally wounded, 9 Officers of the Fusiliers, and God knows how many others. All became confused and had to retreat on the Cabul Gate, which we held from that time. The 3rd Column advanced up the town towards the Jumma Masjid,[1] but from the number of streets and the great protection the houses afforded the Sepoys, who could fire on us without being seen themselves, this Column was also obliged to fall back and took possession of the Church. From the sketch[2] you will see how we were placed, holding but a very small portion of the City, the College on our left and Cabul Gate on the right. The 4th Column, which attacked the suburbs (that wretched Subjhee Mundee, where we lost so many during the siege, and where I was wounded on the 14th July) Goolab Sing's troops[3] were sent in support of this, but they fled the first shot, leaving their guns in the hands of the enemy. This so crippled our men that they had also to retire. The Cavalry and H.A. all this time were creating a diversion outside the Walls, rather a mad act,[4] I think, for they suffered most severely having to retire, and did little or no good so our first start was not very cheering was it? About 12 I got some

[1] The principal Mahomedan mosque.

[2] Missing.

[3] The Kashmir contingent.

[4] Writing with a fuller knowledge, Lord Roberts in his book gives an account of the good work performed by the Cavalry and Horse Artillery on this occasion.

breakfast in the Church, thro' which the round shot were coming pretty fast, and such a number of woebegone faces I think I had never seen before in my life. Every Column had been obliged to retreat. Our best Officer by ten thousand times, poor Nicholson, I had just seen put in a doolie with death on his face, and with the exception of Norman, Johnson and one or two more, no one seemed fit for anything. All the old Officers were completely at their wits' ends. To make matters worse, whether designedly I know not, but the shops with beer and brandy had all been left open, and several of our men got drunk, others could not find their Regiments, and all were done up with the hard work we had had for the previous 5 or 6 days. At last it was determined to remain as we were for the night and see what would turn up in the morning. Nothing could have kept my eyes open, I believe, and as soon as I heard this point settled, I dropped off to sleep, and notwithstanding all the noise, never awoke till sunset. I then went round our position with Norman and Johnson and had a little scrimmage, as I told Mother of in my letter of the 15th. We found all the posts in much the same disorder. No rations had found their way into the town. The poor devils of cook boys could not be persuaded to come in. The fire was so heavy from every corner, Europeans were drunk and natives out plundering. Such an extraordinary scene one is seldom destined to see. However, we cheered all up and told them to hold on till the morning, when all would be right. From the list of casualties, you will at once see what hard fighting we had. The 4 Columns consisted scarcely of 4000 men and Officers—not a very large Force to go at a place like Delhi, but we were getting weaker daily from sickness, and delay would have ruined the whole country. Between the 10th and 14th, while we were breaching we lost about 300, on the 14th 1174, of which 64 were Officers, and up to the 20th, the day on which the town was completely in our possession, about 100 more. Had I been told our loss would have been as much again, I would still have advocated going at it, or we never should. From Peshawur to Delhi, the Musalmans were all ready to rise, and were breaking out here and there, besides the Natives we had with us were getting tired of the fun, and several very shaky to our cause, especially the Artillery Lascars and Magazine Classhees,[1] so we had nothing else to do. I am right glad there was no chance

[1] Inferior artillerymen, tent-pitchers, or sailors. From two Persian words—*Lashkarī*, one attached to, or following, a Lashkar or army; and *Khalāsī*, a sailor or artilleryman.

of assistance from below—or our General (Wilson) would have waited to a certainty, and before any troops could have joined us, our own Force would have been ruined by disease. Since the 8th June, we have lost 4000 men killed and wounded, and upwards of 200 Officers, besides which from cholera we suffered fearfully, and at no time have our numbers been more than 9000 men. Those who have escaped are lucky fellows, and cannot be too thankful. But to my story. On the 15th, parts of the Town were told off to Engineers to try and get the communication extended and advance our posts. They had lost so many Officers that I had a division given to me between the Cabul and Lahore Gates, the part where we had suffered the most severely. I soon found it was impossible to rush ahead. The only chance was to get possession of house after house, and try and command the ramparts between the two gates. This, after the commencement, was not very difficult, and on the evening of the 19th, we were able, by our Riflemen, to keep the rebels out of a strong Bastion (The Burn) between the 2 gates. Hunting about I found a lane with a door exactly opposite the ramp leading up to the Bastion. This answered famously, so as soon as it was dark, I got the Officer commanding the Picquet to bring 50 Europeans and some few Sikhs for the purpose of taking possession of the Work. The soldiers from want of rest and having been beaten back once or twice were, I am sorry to say, anything but eager for a fight. I told them the Bastion was empty, but that a sentry or two might be below who would have to be knocked over. Out we went, and as I thought a few shots were fired right into our faces from some Sepoys under the Walls. This over, all was our own, but to my surprise I found the Officer in Command of the party and myself were the only two present, every other soul had bolted. I went back and spoke to them, not a little disgusted, but I soon got them round, and away we went and took the place as jolly as possible. The next morning we managed to get the Lahore Gate in the same way. I found some 60 old Banias[1] in a house hiding both from fear of the Sepoys and from us. I put a guard over them, and taking a couple made them show me the best road, telling them at the same time if any accident happened to me the others would all be killed. They put me into a room just over the gate, where I saw the scoundrels of Sepoys lolling about and loading a couple of guns, as

[1] *Bania*, a Hindi shopkeeper, grain-dealer, trader, merchant, from the Sanskrit *Vanij*, a merchant.

if they were going to remain masters of Delhi for ever.[1] They were talking about us and seemed quite happy. However, 2 or 3 Riflemen soon dislodged them, and from that moment we never saw a Sepoy again. Within half an hour we walked up the "Chandni Chauk"[2] without seeing a soul, almost to the Palace to where our left had advanced. Powder bags were then brought up, and away went the gates of the Great Mogul. In we all rushed, killing every man we came across, which, however, were but few, and that night Headquarters were moved to the Palace, and we dined in the King's small Durbar room. Everybody was turned out of the City, and all the houses were plundered. A very necessary punishment, but at the same time a sad sight to see old women and little children who had probably never stirred out of their houses before making for one of the gates and leaving their homes. The Sepoys ran off in all directions and several have died on the road. The Pursuing Column could not be started off before it did (the 24th), owing to the great confusion which I fancy must ensue when a small force occupies a large place like Delhi. All our

[1] Part of the City wall, together with the Kabul and Lahore Gates and the Burn Bastion have now disappeared, but the house from which the writer looked down on the Sepoys at the Lahore Gate can still be indentified.

[2] The principal street in Delhi.

best Officers are knocked over, and we are commanded by a muff of a fellow named Greathed, who knows nothing. I am very jolly. In my appointment, 150 Cavalry are attached to me, and with these I go ahead of the Column scouring the whole country. Our present destination is Agra, but we have one or two small Rajahs and Forts to walk into on the road. After Agra, I fancy we shall go towards Rohilkund, and effect a junction somewhere with Havelock's force. Lucknow ought to have been relieved ere this,[1] so we shall have a good army to act whenever necessary. I am so glad I came to Delhi. Such service I may never see again, and I have done my best to profit by it. I have been most favourably mentioned in Despatches, and may get a *Brevet Majority*!! Two years ago I should have been certain of it, but the new rules say that no Subaltern is to be promised a Brevet on promotion. However, there are several Captains who expect to be Majors, and who have not been so well spoken of, besides which, I was selected for this Column, so I think they must give it to me. Norman, for instance, they can never pass over him, and if one

[1] The Force under Generals Havelock and Outram fought its way into Lucknow on September 25, but it suffered such heavy casualties in the advance that the evacuation of the garrison was found to be an impossible task, and the new-comers had to take their part with the besieged. The Residency was not relieved until November.

exception is made, I daresay another will, but the work is not over yet, and altho' we shall never have anything like Delhi again, I may still have opportunities of doing something. Thank God my health is good. I have never been so well, altho' I am perfectly black from exposure to the sun. Nothing seems to knock me up, and this is the chief thing. Do you think Major Fred. Roberts will do? For the present perhaps!! Give my kind love to my own Mother and Harrie, and tell them I will write whenever I can. Dâks may be safe, but the country is so disturbed that I doubt our being able to be certain of them. I have not received any letters from you by the 12th August Mail, but mine, as usual I suppose, have gone to Peshawur. The papers put Hamilton down for 3 months' more leave. I hope he won't come out till quite recovered, and not bring a wife out this time. India is not the place for ladies now. Until civilians have got order and caught some of the thieves that are about the country loose from jail, travelling will not be safe. I have wished the last few days there were no such things as women where war was. Kicking men out of house and home matters little, but I cannot bear seeing unfortunate women suffering, and yet it can't be helped. I must end this long yarn. God bless you all. Fond love to

Innes and John.—Ever believe me, your very affect. son,

FRED. ROBERTS.

After all this is over, I should like to come home and see all you dear ones. Would it not be jolly?

CAMP BULANDSHAHR,
Sept. 30*th*, 1857.
25*th Birthday.*

MY DEAREST MOTHER—I wrote to the General very lately, but as I may not be able to send you a letter for some time after our force leaves this place, and you will probably see in the papers that we have had a fight here and consequently be anxious, I'll write a few lines to-day. My next I have no doubt will go by Calcutta, as before long I hope we shall be in communication with Cawnpore, and from there the road is all safe. On arriving with the Advance Guard here on the morning of the 28th to our surprise we were challenged by an Irregular Cavalry Sowar—it was scarcely morning—and he thought we were his friends. However, before we could lay hold of him he found his mistake out, and was off. We then halted for daybreak, and from one or two villagers ascertained that the enemy were entrenched in a strong position in the Cantonments and were determined to fight. When our troops arrived the H.A. and Cavalry were sent on to open the ball. Presently the Infantry came up and we set to work in earnest. For some time the rascals managed their guns well, but by degrees they were silenced and we advanced nearer. Our force of Infantry is small and the few Europeans we have are thoroughly done up with exposure and sickness. However, the Artillery and Cavalry came on, and we captured a gun, at which I got up to first. Upon this the enemy retreated and away we went after them, cutting up a good many and recovering lots of plunder they were carrying off. On our return I accompanied a squadron of the 9th Lancers, and on going through a nasty street in the city a strong body of the enemy, who had been concealed in houses, made a stand and opened a heavy fire on us. We charged, and I had the misfortune to have a very fine charger shot right between his eyes—lucky his head was in the way or I should have caught it—and as we were only a few yards off, I have no doubt it would have inflicted a very nasty wound. It was the first morning I had ever ridden him—a favourite horse of poor General Nicholson's, which I bought after his death. The poor brute is still alive, but in a very bad way, so

I have now 2 horses *hors de combat*. A great nuisance, for it is impossible to get others. I fortunately started with 4. Early in the day, the old charger had a very narrow escape. A round shot came lobbing along and passed between his legs! Rather close. The end of the affair was that we licked the scoundrels out of the place, took 2 guns and no end of ammunition. That same evening a strong fort which we had come expressly to storm was evacuated, our friends having had enough fighting. I am glad they left of their own accord, as our force is small, and in the fight of the 28th we lost 50 men, and would certainly have suffered severely in taking the fort. The wounded go into Meerut to-night or to-morrow, and we start for Aligarh and Agra. I hope by the 1st November to be at Cawnpore, unless we are sent into Rohilkund, which is very possible as it is there the Mutineers have all fled to, so you may not hear very regularly, my own Mother, from me. The Brevet Majority is looking up I think! Our Brigadier mentioned me very handsomely in his Despatch yesterday. Jolly is it not? Then when I come home and see you all, how happy we will be. I could not have missed this service for anything; such a chance I may never have again. Hitherto, I have been most mercifully preserved, and if all goes well to the end I shall be a fortunate fellow. I am just as good as "pukha"[1] in the Quartermaster-General's Department, and am sure of not being turned out again. So, my Mother, I think I am indeed a lucky fellow. This is my 25th Birthday. I am sure you are thinking of me. How can I ever thank you for all you have done? But for your kind care and affection, I should never have got on, and I can well remember what trouble I used to give you, but you must not think of that Mother now, only of my love for and extreme gratitude to you. My chief pleasure in doing well is knowing that it will make you and the General proud and happy. I only wish I could hear from you oftener. No letters by the 10th August Mail. None come yet and I hear that the dâks between Mooltan and Lahore have been looted, so that my letters have probably gone with others. I hope not, however, for once a fortnight nowadays seems seldom eno' to hear, and it is just possible they may turn up yet after paying a visit to Peshawur. News has just come from Aligarh that the rebels have taken possession of the Fort and intend holding out. From all accounts it is a very strong place, but out of repair, and as they cannot

[1] *Pukka*, a Hindi word meaning ripe, mature, cooked, and hence substantial, permanent; the opposite of *kachcha*, meaning raw, crude, uncooked, hence temporary.

Mrs Roberts

From a sketch by Carpenter

have many guns or much ammunition, I do not imagine we shall have much difficulty in turning them, should they wait for our arrival, which I doubt. What nonsense *The Times* talks about the Mutiny being confined to the Army. In this district there never was an Army. Some 60 Sepoys formed the Garrison, and yet it has behaved as bad if not worse than any other. With scarcely an exception, all the Police and Native Civil Authorities joined at the very commencement, and the many independent Rajahs raised their Standards against us. Every villager tore down European houses and robbed their property. Fortunately for us, they are such a despicable set of cowards that they bury their faces in the dirt the moment we show ourselves, and ask for pardon. For a year or two, I would like to have charge of some very bad district to see if I could not break them in. Our civilians have ruined India by not punishing natives sufficiently, and by allowing all the rascals in the country to hold high offices in their Kutcherries.[1] Poor Nicholson was the man.[2] His was an iron rule, and such a district you never saw, every villain

[1] *Kutcheri* or *Kachheri*, a Hindi word meaning a court or office of public business.

[2] Nicholson was worshipped as a saint by some of the men on the frontier; they formed themselves into a sect, and called themselves "Nicholseyns."

was known and, of course, led a life of misery, while the good men found out the advantage of speaking the truth and being honest. However, we have military law now, which helps to keep people quiet. Tell dearest Harrie I will write to her next Mail in answer to all her nice kind letters. I am so glad you have enjoyed your visit to Aunt Hunter. Give her my very kind love. Lind I left behind at Delhi. He is a fine dashing fellow, but too quick in his temper and not sufficiently thoughtful ever to be a first-rate Officer. His likeness to Lizzie is perfectly absurd. It is so sad to find among the traps of the rebel Sepoys all sorts of ladies' dresses, work, jewellery, likenesses, etc., etc. Poor unfortunate creatures, how they must have suffered, and what on earth these wretches intended doing with them, I can't make out. I picked up the other day a very handsome black net dress with red trimmings, black satin slip—in fact all complete—crumpled up in a Sepoy's bedding. It was no use, so I burnt it, as I could not bear to look at it, and to think to what happy, pretty girl it might have belonged. I wish much —— had been on this service, only not in the Commissariat Department. One can never win honour or glory in that. I would infinitely prefer working a gun to such an appointment, and I expect to hear that Officers will not be allowed to remain in it, but that a somewhat similar establishment to Filder & Co. will be introduced into this country. It is very pretty about here, such trees and gardens, so different from the Punjab, yet I prefer the climate of the latter, and will return to Peshawur with great pleasure when all is over, spend 2 or 3 years there and then go home and see you, my own Mother. What a delightful prospect to think my fun has to come, and that I have not yet taken my furlough! But take it I will, please God, whatever appointment I hold when my time is up. Good-bye. With my fondest love to the General, Harrie, Innes, John and Hamilton, if with you.—Ever believe me, my own dearest Mother, your very affect. attached son,

FRED. ROBERTS.

CAMP NEAR AGRA,
Oct. 15th, 1857.

MY DEAREST MOTHER—Since I wrote to you on the 30th ult., we have travelled thus far and had two more fights, one at Aligarh on the 5th, and the second at Agra on the 10th. On arriving at the former place early in the morning, we found the City held by insurgents, and as I rode on with a few cavalry, just to get a glimpse at them, a shot of defiance came in amongst us, plainly showing that resistance was intended.

I sent a note back for assistance, and remained quietly looking on. Some time elapsed ere 2 H.A. guns could be brought up, and the rascals came out of the city hooting at us and flourishing their swords, dragging along a couple of guns from which every now and then they took a shot at us, but without doing much damage. Just as they got well in the open, the H.A. came up and with a couple of rounds sent our friends flying back to the city, leaving the guns with us. In the city they might have held out for ever, but after an hour's scrimmaging, they took to their heels. Luckily we hit upon the right road and followed them up. I had just mounted a fresh horse when the pursuit commenced, so none could get ahead of me. After going down the Cawnpore road some 4 miles we overtook their Cavalry. I looked round for the 9th Lancers, but after the long march, their horses could not stand the pace, and I found only some 20 Sikhs near me. At them we went, and I don't think one got away. On our return we polished off the Infantry, and left altogether about 400 on the field with a very slight loss to ourselves. The next day, the 6th, we made one march towards Cawnpore to a village called "Akberabad" where two rascals lived who had set themselves up as Rajahs. This was a very slight affair, and we were intending to go down the trunk Road to join Havelock's force in Lucknow, when express after express came from Agra asking us to hurry over as they were in daily expectation of being attacked by the Gwalior troops.[1] The H.A. and Cavalry started first and marched to within 10 miles of the Fort, until the Infantry came up, when we all went into Agra on the morning of the 10th, having marched 46 miles in 30 hours. I marked out the ground for encamping on the Brigade Parade, and then started off to enquire the news about the mutineers. All the Civil and Military Authorities in the Fort assured me that from the latest intelligence they had received, the Pandies had fled hearing of our approach, and recrossed a stream about 10 miles off on the Gwalior Road. With this information I returned to Camp, determining not to reconnoitre the country until the evening, as I imagined such swells must have proper intelligence. However, that they had been deceived was very soon evident. Round shot after round shot came whizzing thro' our tents, only a few of which luckily were pitched, owing to the long march—the greater part of the baggage was in the rear. We turned out and our guns were brought to bear in the direction

[1] The Gwalior Contingent was composed of troops raised in the State of the Maharajah Scindia and officered by British officers. The Maharajah had warned the authorities that the general disaffection had spread to its ranks.

of the enemy's (it was impossible to see anything but their smoke on account of the high cultivation) while the Cavalry and Infantry formed up in support. We were scarcely in position when some 600 or 700 rascally Sowars came rushing round both our flanks and making steadily for the rear. You may imagine the confusion—baggage strewed over the ground, servants flying everywhere, and no Commanding Officer to be found. On our right the Sowars met their match in the 3 squadrons of Punjab Cavalry, and got well pitched into, but on our left we had only the 9th Lancers, and altho' they are magnificent men and first-rate for a charge, they scarcely can cope with native horsemen in single combat. One of our guns unfortunately was disabled, having two horses just knocked over, and this the rascals surrounded before assistance could be rendered. They cut the gunners down but were soon made to disgorge their prize by a charge from the 9th Lancers, who immediately afterwards made another fine charge and drove the main body off. A few stragglers remained, and with these some very pretty single combats took place. In the confusion at first my horses had been led away and I only found a pony to ride. Mounted on this I did not feel quite sure about tackling an Irregular Cavalryman. However, one came dancing about me, so I thought I would try my revolver. Altho' one of Deane & Adams' very best, it missed fire at each barrel and I had barely time to draw my sword when we closed. I fortunately managed to get on my friend's wrong side and rolled him with a knock on his head ere he could do me any damage. The great thing I have found in all cases of this sort, is a horse over which you have perfect control. My two chargers are first-rate, fiery, swift and brave, but I can manage them completely and mounted on either of them I dread no Sowar. A pony is a different affair, and the treacherous pistol nearly cost me my life. However, "all's well that ends well," and at the moment my fun was over, up went one of the enemy's ammunition wagons. Our line then advanced. We soon came across an immense brass gun, which was captured. Up goes another wagon, and the day is ours. We pursued the Pandies for 10 miles to the banks of the stream, taking 12 *guns*, all their baggage and camp equipage, and killing some 600 or 700 of the scoundrels. I never enjoyed a gallop more, seeing the wretched Sepoys first of all as you neared them throw away all their loot, then their arms and running as hard as they could, a few died like men, but the greater part begged for mercy. One villain, as I was coming close upon him with a spear seized a child from a woman close by and used it as a shield. I, however, managed to spear him and saved the poor little babe. This was the end of the Agra affair. We returned home just at dark, having gone nearly 70 miles in 40 hours, besides fighting a severe action. I don't remember ever being so tired before in my life. The fort at Agra is such an extraordinary sight, filled with people of every colour, altogether 6000, of which 125 are ladies. From having been so long shut out from all communication with other places, many have become most terribly selfish, and fancy Agra is the one place in India. The Chief Commissioner, a Colonel Fraser, of the Engineers, did all he could to keep our Column there, altho' he knew perfectly that, without it, the troops down country could do but little, as they have no Artillery or Cavalry. Nothing could happen to Agra. The Cantonments have been destroyed ages ago, but the fort is strong enough to keep any number of Pandies off, and they have provisions stored for 11 months, long ere which time I hope we shall be on our way back, having thrashed the Pandies out of house and home. Yet there are a few nice people still left. Some old Peshawur friends who gave us *two picnics*!! at the Taj. What a lovely place the Taj is. I have never seen anything like it, perfect in every way. We had it lighted up. The more you look at it, the better pleased you are. How glorious the designer must have felt when the means for bringing into reality what his wonderful imagination had conjured up were placed at his disposal. I could have spent days and days there. However, I had two very pleasant evenings. Heroes from Delhi! are thought something of, and the poor creatures in the fort were only glad of the opportunity of getting a little fresh air. I breakfasted one morning with an old friend of the General's, George Harvey of the Civil Service. He gave me great assistance in procuring Natives for information, and I'll bet that our camp is not surprised as we were at Agra. In writing my report about the business, I took care to mention how it occurred, otherwise great blame might have been attached to me.[1] Your dear letter of the 7th and Harrie's of the 17th I received a few days ago. My own Mother, I am so glad to hear from you. Travelling about in these outlandish places, I seem to be so far from you, and yet my next letter will, I fancy, go *viâ* Calcutta, as I shall not have an opportunity of writing until we arrive at Cawnpore.

[1] This report is given in the Appendix, page 163.

Once we join the Commander-in-Chief, our route lies up thro' Rohilkund, so I shall see the business out, if God spares my life. What a lucky fellow I am, coming from Peshawur and being present at every action except one or two of the early ones before Delhi. I want to hear about the Medals. We should have one for Delhi alone, but the Government in this country affect to treat the matter lightly, and until the other day had never issued one single order of thanks, neither have any despatches been published, but they must do what is just, so I shall probably get 2 Medals! Give my best love and congratulations to dearest Innes on the birth of her little boy. I would write to her, but I have little spare time, and one long letter every Mail will do for you all. So Hamilton is going to be married. Give him my love also and wish him every happiness. How I shall long to go home and see you all after this is all over. I may then perhaps find a Mrs. Roberts. Tell dear Innes I drank her health on the 9th, and will wish old Hamilton all success in a bumper on the 21st. Poor Fidget[1] died last December, but I have a son of his named "Faust" which Hamilton shall look at. If I have a chance, I will certainly pay Calcutta a visit and get brushed up before returning to

[1] A dog.

Peshawur, and also go to Simla or Missourie for a month or two and stay with the Boisragons.

Good-bye, my own dearest Mother. With fondest love to the General and Harrie.—Ever your affect. attached son,

FRED. ROBERTS.

We shall be at Cawnpore about the 1st prox.

CAMP, CAWNPORE,
Oct. 27*th*, 1857.

MY DEAREST MOTHER—I wrote to you from Agra on the 14th *viâ* Bombay, since which time the Column has moved down the Trunk road to this. We met with but little opposition, took "Mainpuri" without a shot, and established a horse dâk to the juncture of the two roads from Aligarh and Agra. After this, we placed runners, and up till to-day the post has come regularly. Unfortunately, we could not spare any men to hold a station between this and Agra, and I have just heard that the Nawab of Fatehgarh has killed a Cassid and blocked up the road so I fear our communication is cut off again. One morning we had a little fight at a village called "Kunoj." I had received information of 4 guns guarded by 300 or 400 men being there, but that they would be probably removed as we approached.

However, when nearing the City, my spies informed me the enemy were within 2 miles of the encamping ground and trying to get the guns over a stream. I had some 20 Sowars, so galloped down, sending back word to the Advance Guard to come up as fast as they could with 2 guns and some Cavalry. My rapid advance had the effect of making the enemy leave 1 gun on this side, in their hurry to save themselves. The other 3 were already across the stream, and with one of them, while I was taking a look thro' the "Binoculars," they fired a round of grape, which knocked over my orderly's horse and wounded me slightly in the face, very nearly carrying off my whisker!! At this time, the 2 guns came up, and after 3 or 4 rounds sent the rascals scampering leaving their guns behind. The cavalry then crossed over, and we had a famous gallop driving the rebels, after a 6 miles' run, *into the Ganges*!! I only saw one man reach the other side, and one horse, very few got off. Some of the Infantry hid in the cultivation and escaped. I, as usual, had a horse wounded by a sabre cut. A dismounted Sowar aimed at me. I guarded the blow, saved myself, but my poor nag got a sad cut. However, it was a very good affair, and I got mentioned for getting so quickly on the fellows and making them leave a gun behind. We arrived here yesterday. I came in the day before. Such a sight as Cawnpore is, you would never know it, Mother. The place where Sir H. Wheeler defended himself is the most perfect ruin from round shot that I have ever seen—2 small barracks with an apology of a ditch, not eno' to keep a bullet out, —such lamentable infatuation. They say poor Wheeler was afraid to build himself a strong position for fear of exciting suspicion amongst the natives, and in this wretched place, our poor women were exposed for 3 weeks to the fearful sun of June at Cawnpore, and the shot of the enemy whose batteries were erected about 200 yds. off. Many ladies were killed, others wounded. The survivors were kept in a miserable house, not fit for dogs, until the evening before our troops reached Cawnpore, when they were all murdered. God only knows how. The natives say that the children were hanged before their mothers, and that when all had been wounded by shots from the Sepoys, butchers were sent in to finish the bloody business. There were about 200 altogether—women and children. The floor now is strewed with clothes, shoes, etc., and the ground from the house to the well, where the remains were thrown down, is covered with locks of hair. Oh, Mother, looking at these horrible sights makes one feel very, very sad. No wonder we all feel glad to kill these Sepoys. What the unfortunate women and children must have suffered. I trust the massacres are all over. Yet, in Lucknow, they are in a bad way. Havelock's Force saved the Garrison from the imminent danger they were in, but he himself is now surrounded with the others by the rebel army, and has written in here to say that, with the strictest economy, the Commissariat Officer has reported that the flour for bread, and bullocks (formerly *used to drag the guns*) will only last till the 10*th November*, by which date, unless we relieve them, they will either starve or give themselves up. Our force is not very strong, but we receive here about 500 fresh Infantry, making the Column consist of 2000 Infantry (half of which are Sikhs), 750 Cavalry and 16 light guns. With this we leave on the 31st, and make our advanced post in 3 marches. This post is 5 miles from the Residency where our people are, the ladies living underground, but all communication between the 2 posts is cut off. At this place we leave the road and make our way round to the East where the canal joins the river. All the bridges over the canal are broken, and we have to cut our way. Once across we shall be about 2 miles from Havelock, and at the appointed signal, the two forces advance to meet each other. This is the present plan, but thousands of accidents may prevent it. However, happen what will, we must reach the inside ere the 10th. Our stores alone will require a small army to protect them, but with God's help all will come right. Who would have thought the Delhi force would assist Lucknow? Two months ago, we were anxiously looking out for Havelock's arrival in our camp at Delhi. It is impossible to make a guess even at the number of rebels we may have to oppose. Oude teems with Sepoys. All from Delhi have fled there, and I hear they have some 150 guns. A month hence we could go with an enormous force, but the delay of a week would be ruination, so at it we must, and I anticipate perfect success. The Commander-in-Chief has telegraphed that he will be here by the 1st or 2nd, and will overtake us. Here is my good luck, being with his part of the force, and with which, if possible, I will remain. Norman will do his best to keep me, and if I succeed, I shall be all right. They took it into their heads that I was hard worked, so offered me an assistant, and I have got a very nice fellow of my own Regiment, and an old friend of mine, named Mayne. He is far above me, being

12 years' service, but very glad indeed, he says, to serve under me. Rather fun is it not? I have not really very much work to do, beyond a good deal of riding and being kept always on the *qui vive* about information, —different from other campaigns—civilians and politicals have nothing to do, so I have the whole work of the column.[1] The rebels from Gwalior are at "Kalpee," over the Jumna, where they have just finished a bridge of boats, but what they intend doing it is difficult to say. I doubt much their coming to Cawnpore. However, we wait till the 31st to see their route and then cross the Ganges into Oude. . . . We shall have some work, but I have great faith in the Delhi troops. They are steady, at least the Artillery and Cavalry are, and we have one or two good men. It is so odd the way fellows turn out. Many who in a station appeared great swells, do nothing on service and *vice versa*. How jolly it will be when all is over, coming to see you, dearest Mother, with medals for "Delhi" and "Lucknow." I have been promised to be recommended for a Cavalry Corps, but I would far

[1] When a campaign is undertaken by the Government of India the Force is always accompanied by a Political Officer whose duty is to get into touch with the people of the country in which operations are carried on, and to keep the Government and the General in Command of the Force informed on all matters not strictly military.

rather remain as I am. . . . Besides, there is nothing like the general staff, altho' the pay may not be so good. I went over Wheeler's entrenchment again this morning, and picked up a couple of sheets of music with Innes' song "*Non giova il sospirar!*" There is scarcely a foot left on the walls where a cannon shot has not struck—one Officer who escaped showed me spots where Officers and ladies had been killed while leaning against the walls. Wheeler of the 1st N.I. had been wounded, his sister was fanning him, when a ball came and took his head off. You see places where mothers had scraped away the floor to make hollows for their babes to sleep in. No words can express one's feelings while going over these horrid places. At Lucknow, amongst the ladies, is Mrs. Hayes (Fanny Torrens that was). The 93rd Highlanders marched in this morning, looking so nice in the kilts. The natives think they are the ghosts of the murdered women, but the sailors astonish them most—"4 ft. high, 4 ft. broad, long hair, and dragging big guns!!" They can't make them out. This goes *viâ* Calcutta. After "Lucknow" has been relieved, I will write again, my own Mother. Hamilton I suppose is thinking about starting for this delightful country again. I hope I may see him after the work is all over. I shall try and pay Calcutta a visit, just to get brushed up and have my beard trimmed! I am afraid the "Royals" will have it all their own way now. It will be a shame if they don't reward and increase our Regiment. We have lost about 40 Officers since May, but our good men are all gone—Nicholson, Neill,[1] etc., and Queen's Officers command everywhere. However, I suppose it will all come right in the end. I long more than ever to go home and see you all. These last few months have made me feel 10 years older, not from bad health, for I have never been so well, but from all that I have seen and undergone. One can't help thinking and reflecting on these unparalleled massacres. Soldiers know what their fate may be, but one can scarcely understand why delicate women and helpless children have been made to undergo such tortures. God bless them. It makes me quite sad writing about them. Mrs. Norman has collected passages from Norman's letters which she is sending home to his mother, and has asked her to forward them on to the General, as Norman and I were constantly together during the siege, and they will give you a better account than my letters written once a

[1] Brigadier-General James Neill, killed in Lucknow, September 1857.

fortnight. Give my kind love to dear Innes. I am so glad to hear her little baby is flourishing. Write to me, Mother, *long*, *long* letters every Mail. My one must do for all, as I know you will forward it on to Innes and John. I am in great trouble about my horses. The two wounded ones won't get well, and the third is very C.D. No money will buy horses now—none are to be had, and I must ride, so it is as bad as a Chinese puzzle. I should like very much a brace of pistols, what they call "*over and under*," not too large. I don't care how unfinished as long as the locks are good. These revolvers, I am convinced, are of little use. Mine always fails me. Good-bye, Mother. Best love to the General and darling Harrie.—Ever, my own Mother, your very affect. and attached son,

FRED. ROBERTS.

CAMP'S MARCH FROM LUCKNOW,
Nov. 1st, 1857.

MY DEAREST FATHER—I am afraid you may think from the letter I wrote to Mother while at Cawnpore that I am in low spirits. It was, I remember, a dismal jemmy sort of an affair, but in that wretched station where such atrocities had been committed, I could not feel happy. Now we are out of it and well on our way to be revenged on the very fiends who perpetrated those unheard-of cruelties, and I feel as jolly as possible. To-morrow we reach "Alambagh," a strong position about 4 miles on this side of the Residency, where we have a post. There we halt one day in the hopes that Sir Colin may arrive, and there we leave our tents and baggage, proceeding in light order to the S.E. of the City, where we are to endeavour to cross the canal, and fight our way to Havelock's Garrison, holding positions as we advance, so as to be able to bring the ladies, etc., away without risk. This achieved, and with the female portion in Alambagh we shall be able to send them into Cawnpore by degrees, and at the same time to thrash our friends out of Lucknow. Am I not a fortunate fellow to be Quartermaster-General to a force destined for such a glorious object. All the Intelligence Department is in my hands. In my wildest dreams I never thought of what was so soon to happen, and when next I write I hope to tell you that I am in the Department permanently. If possible, I shall try and remain with Head-quarters, as I imagine Sir Colin will see the business to an end. However, if he deputes the "Hero of the Redan"[1] or any one else to follow up into Rohilkund, I shall do my

[1] Major-General Windham, C.B.

best to go on too. The only drawback to the business is not getting our dâks. The English letters of the 10th Sept. are, I am afraid, all lost. The very day the post was destroyed near Mainpuri I expected to have heard from some of you, and since then nothing has come. I sent men back to see if they could recover the bags anywhere, but nothing has been heard of them. Is not this disgusting? The only letters I want to receive. However, it can't be helped, and ere this day month, I hope we shall have troops at every station South of Agra. Before leaving Cawnpore, a company of Royal Artillery joined us. The first fellow I saw was "Hardy," who formerly lived at Clifton, looking very well. Advancing on Lucknow, we shall have a force of 1800 European Infantry, and 900 Native ditto, about 300 European Cavalry and 350 Native ditto, 16 light and 4 heavy guns, and with this we ought, and will, please God, lick Pandy well, altho' I believe they are immense numbers, and are joined by some 40,000 fanatic Musalmans, chiefly retainers of the ex-King, whose wife we hear English ladies go to see in crowds, and actually kneel to kiss her hands. This surely can't be true? Altho' I believe curiosity will overcome much to be gratified. I can't help thinking of Hamilton having to leave old

England and all you dear ones. How sad he must be. I shall try all I can to see him, and, if necessary, will pay a visit to Calcutta ere the hot weather commences. I long so to hear about you and hope he brings me out your likeness, and also dear "Harrie's." Indeed, I want one of all,—Mother, Innes, John and the children. Daguerreotypes are so simple now and no trouble, so that if you have not sent them by Hamilton, do so in a little box to Allen & Deffell. I can't tell you how much I shall prize them. Give my kind love to Harriet Roberts (Mrs. Tom) and tell her I will write next Mail, but that I have not time this, indeed, I have very little time for anything, and am seldom out of the saddle. Norman and I share the same tent. He, poor fellow, got a bad kick a few days ago, and I reap the advantage of it by having his horses to ride, mine, unfortunately, being all sick. However, I think they are getting better. Nothing like change of air for man or beast. I have never been so well thro' cold, heat, or wet. All seems the same, and right thankful am I, for without good health, I could never do my work. What a beautiful country Oude is. All this part of the world is like a park, yet I would rather live in the dusty Punjab, and far prefer the climate of the latter. The heat is greater for a few months, but then you have cold weather. Here, even now, it is very hot. I will write again next Mail, and tell you all about our doings at Lucknow. With my fondest love to Mother, Harrie, and all. Accept the same from your very affect. son,

FRED. ROBERTS.

CAMP "ALAMBAGH,"
Nov. 13th, 1857.

MY DEAREST MOTHER—It may be some days ere I shall have an opportunity of writing to you again, so I'll send a few lines off to-day. I wrote to you from Cawnpore and to the General a day or two after we left that horrid station. On the 2nd or 3rd I wrote to Mrs. Tom, giving her an account of a wonderful escape I had from the Pandies, all of which I hope you have received. I never felt so rejoiced in my life as when I found myself clear of the rascals and near our own men. For some minutes I gave up all hope, but my little grey carried me most beautifully, and I just managed to get round their flank in time. My horse got a nasty cut in his leg, and I one on my left hand. However, both are doing well. We came here yesterday, having been joined a day or two previously by Sir Colin Campbell, and to-morrow we go on to Lucknow. These Pandies are certainly queer fellows. On the line of march yesterday, they commenced firing on us with 2 guns, which, of course, we took at once, and killed all near them, but what they could mean, I can't understand—attacking our force with a couple of miserable guns. Here we leave our tents and spare baggage, taking with us only what is actually necessary, and will halt to-morrow I fancy near the Canal, about 2 miles to the right of the Residency, where our people are besieged. The difficulty will be crossing the Canal. All the bridges are broken and the banks about 25 ft. high. However, we have sufficient heavy Artillery to erect a good battery on this side, under cover of which the work must be done. Once across, we then set to and will have some distance of suburb and street to get thro' ere we can reach Outram's Force. All the way we shall have to occupy posts, under protection of which the women, children and other "impedimenta" will have to be taken to the canal, or wherever our reserve may be, and then we shall make our way back to Cawnpore. The whole country of Oude is against us, and any force that we could leave in Lucknow would be in a state of siege, so I fancy we shall content ourselves by destroying any strong work they have and coming away, until such time as a strong Army can go and remain. Oude is covered with little Forts, one of which we took this morning called "Jellalabad." Until these are destroyed and the population disarmed, nothing will settle down. We shall be in the Residency, please God, by the 15th or 16th. All are well there, as we learnt yesterday by means of a telegraph erected on the top of "Alambagh," which can be seen from the Residency, where they have a similar one, distance about 5 miles. This completely floors the Pandies, as we can now make our arrangements to act in concert, and their Cavalry have rendered any kind of letters being sent in a matter of great difficulty. Sir Colin is looking very well, and for his age wonderfully active.[1] By great exertion he has managed to collect here a very nice force consisting of 16 guns, H.A. Guns (Bengal), 4 heavy 24 mortars (R. Artillery), 8 heavy guns (Naval Brigade), 9th Lancers—350 men, Punjab Cavalry—400 men, a large Park of Engineers formed of Royal, Bengal and Madras Sappers, and the following Regiments of Infantry, including, of course, all the troops belonging to the Column from Delhi:

---

[1] He was sixty-five years of age.

3rd Fusiliers[1]	300
8th Foot	350
53rd „	600
93rd „	1000
Detachments of various Corps, 64th, 78th, 90th & Madras Fus.	1000
	3250
Besides which we have Punjab Infantry . .	800
	4050

A very nice Force is it not? and when we get all that Havelock has with him in Lucknow, say 2000 effective men, and the garrison of 1000 men we leave in Alambagh. We shall reach Cawnpore with a large Army. Troops from Calcutta are arriving there daily, so the occupation of all the stations on the right of the Ganges between Meerut and Cawnpore will I hope be effected by Xmas. At present our dâks are cut off, and no communication takes place except *viâ* Bombay!! or a strange Cassid, who now and then turns up, so the consequence is that I have not heard from you my own darling Mother, since Harrie's letter of the 17th August, and 2 mails have arrived since. I hope the Postmaster at Agra will keep our letters, and

[1] Now the 2nd Royal Sussex Regiment; the King's (Liverpool Regiment); the 1st Shropshire Light Infantry; the 2nd Argyll and Sutherland Highlanders; the 1st North Staffordshire Regiment; the 2nd Seaforth Highlanders; the 2nd Scottish Rifles, and the Dublin Fusiliers.

that I shall receive them eventually. Norman, I think, is certain of being Deputy-Adjutant-General of the Army. Sir Colin has a great opinion of him, and he certainly is one of the finest fellows in India. In these times of work, I don't like applying to be put permanently into the Quartermaster-General's Department, but will do so as soon as I can. However, I am sure of it, and if I cannot remain with the Headquarters of the Army, will try and get sent with the Column that marches up country against Fatehgarh, etc., and then return to my old quarters at Peshawur. However, I would prefer remaining with the Commander-in-Chief, and think I have a good chance of doing so. The nights are a little too cold now, particularly sleeping outside, but one would go thro' anything on a service of this sort. Fancy the joy of the poor ladies a day or two hence when they see us, for altho' they have managed to get bread and meat sufficient to live on, how they must have suffered—no milk, sugar, tea or anything they have been used to, and most of them with young children. Mrs. Hayes is all well. I shall be very glad to see her, but she will scarcely remember "Master Freddie" in the bearded, sunburnt individual he has become. Fancy sailors at Lucknow! Such jolly looking fellows and ready for anything. Well, good-bye, Mother. Give my kind love to the General, Harrie, Innes and John, and ever believe me, my own darling Mother, your very affect. son,

FRED. ROBERTS.

Hamilton, I suppose, has left ere this.

CAMP NEAR LUCKNOW,
Nov. 25*th*, 1857.

MY DEAREST MOTHER—You will be glad to hear from me an account of our doings at Lucknow, and of my getting safely thro' the affair. We left this place "Alambagh" on the 14th, leaving our tents, etc., behind, and marched to a place called Dilkusha, N.E. of the City, where we came across the enemy, but soon drove them down the Hill to the Martinière,[1] from where they opened on us with heavy Artillery. After some banging on both sides, our Infantry advanced, took the Martinière and occupied the adjoining

[1] The Martinière was built by Claude Martin, a French soldier of fortune who came to India under the Comte de Lally in 1757. When peace was made with the French, he enlisted in the East India Company's Army, and was allowed to attach himself to the court of the King of Oude, where he obtained great influence and amassed a large fortune. He founded colleges at Lucknow, Calcutta, and Lyons, his native town. His directions that his house at the former place should never be sold, but should "serve as a college for educating children and men in the English language and religion" were carried out by the British Government. The Martinière is still a college, and Martin lies buried in its vault.

ground. It was night ere we finished fighting, and as none of our traps had come up we had to lie down on the ground, some lucky eno' to get a little dinner, but many having to go without. The next morning, the 15th, was spent in getting the troops together, issuing rations, etc., etc. This took so long that it was determined not to commence operations on the City until the 16th. After breakfast on the 16th therefore, we started again, crossing the canal near the river, and making for a strong place called the "Sekundarbagh," we soon came upon it, and found the enemy in great numbers. The way we went up exposed us to a heavy fire on 3 sides, and how our Artillery escaped I can't imagine. Sir Colin was first everywhere and brought the guns up, but they could not silence the heavy musketry which was streaming out from every inch of the building, so the Highlanders and Sikhs were ordered to storm. It was beautiful to see them going at it, regularly racing to see who should be first in. They went, and before half an hour was over, nearly 2000 Pandies were on the ground dead or dying. I never saw such a sight. They were literally in heaps, and when I went in were a heaving mass, some dead, but most wounded and unable to get up from the crush.

How so many got crowded together I can't understand. You had to *walk over them* to cross the court. They showed their hatred even while dying, cursed us and said: "if we could only stand, we would kill you." That evening, we took 3 or 4 more places and bivouacked for the night. The next day we advanced quietly, and ere evening came into communication with the Garrison. Sir J. Outram and General Havelock came out to see Sir Colin, and Norman and I went inside. During the next day, all the wounded were brought out of the entrenchment and taken to the Dilkusha. The ladies, women, etc., followed on the 19th. The 20th, 21st, and 22nd were occupied in bringing out stores, destroying guns, etc., and before morning on the 23rd we had all left the city and returned to the Martinière. Sir Colin managed everything famously, but we suffered heavily. About 500 men and some 50 Officers killed and wounded. Amongst the latter, my old friend Mayne who was acting in the Quartermaster-General's Dept. He was shot dead on the 14th. Poor Hardy was also killed by a round shot on the 16th. It makes one very sad seeing all these fine fellows knocked over. I have lost so many friends during the last 6 months, and at times can't help feeling very very miserable. The constant excitement we have had prevents one thinking, but a quiet day now and then brings back vividly all the horrors that have taken place. One or two ladies I knew well have been killed in this wretched Oude, whose fate until a few days ago I did not know of. The garrison itself suffered but little from sickness, but, of course, 5 months' imprisonment on short rations has told more or less on them all. They can scarcely believe they are free, and undergo their present hardships cheerfully. We marched here yesterday—1 Division with all the women, etc.—but as our tents are limited, many have to remain night and day in their carriages. I found Mrs. Hayes out, and made my tent over to her and some of her friends, so she is in great luck, but I shall be glad when we land them all safely at Cawnpore, for poor women are certainly not suited for camp life in time of war. The C. in Chief brought a Colonel Biddulph with him from Calcutta as head of the Intelligence Department. He was killed poor fellow in Lucknow, and I was appointed to succeed him, so am a great swell. I like Sir Colin, General Mansfield[1] and all the Headquarter people very much, and shall

[1] Brigadier-General Sir William Mansfield, Chief of the Staff to Sir Colin Campbell, afterwards General Lord Sandhurst, G.C.B., G.C.S.I.

try to remain with them if I can. They talk of spending the hot weather at Meerut, which will do for me very nicely, as I shall require a little rest after all this knocking about. The last ten days we had very hard work, and constant exposure night and day. Consequently I am feeling a little C.D., but will be all right in a day or two.

30th, CAWNPORE.—I have never been able to finish this, owing to the incessant marching about, and am almost afraid now that it will not go by this mail, owing to our communication being cut off. On the 27th, we left Alambagh, taking with us 1400 sick and wounded, and 500 women and children, Outram's division remaining behind, as a proof to Pandy that we intended reoccupying Lucknow on some future occasion. Sir C. Napier's opinion of Outram was true in every item. He is no soldier, and I should say no politician.[1] The whole business from Cawnpore to Lucknow, for which he and poor Havelock got so much praise, was simply disgraceful. Nearly all

[1] The writer's connection with General Hunter (see p. 9), who took Sir Charles Napier's part in the well-known controversy between Napier and Outram in Scinde, probably accounts for this boyish criticism. Lord Roberts's admiration for General Outram was very real, and it is interesting to compare this letter with the chapter in *Forty-One Years in India*, in which, with a fuller knowledge of the difficulties encountered by their small force, he speaks of the "Bayard of India" and Havelock, the "hero of a hundred fights."

their wounded were left behind in the streets and cut up. Those that reached the Residency were in a state of disorderly flight, and as they brought no provisions were but an encumbrance to the garrison, who could have subsisted till the end of the year, added to which, we received letters as I may have told you, day after day, urging our rapid advance for fear of their being starved, and our whole force is actually living on the grain we brought out of their camp.[1] Poor Havelock died the day before we left. He was quite done up and fit for nothing. Well, to my story. On the evening of the 27th, we halted at "Bani." Heavy firing in the direction of Cawnpore had been heard for two days, so the next morning Sir Colin determined to push on and reach the river if possible, 30 miles off, and with our impedimenta in the shape of sick and women, no easy task. However, we managed it, and about an hour before sunset, I, who had been sent ahead with some Cavalry, arrived at the Bridge of Boats, and found that all the rebel troops from Gwalior were occupying the station, having

[1] When the disturbances in Oudh first began, the wise precaution of Sir Henry Lawrence led to his laying in a large store of provisions in the Residency, but the Commissariat Officer was severely wounded early in the day and incapacitated during the greater part of the siege, and it was only by degrees that some of the supplies were discovered. When Outram urged on Sir Colin Campbell the necessity for speedy relief on account of the shortage of food, he must have been unaware of the amount still available.

driven our troops back twice, and finally driving them into the entrenchment. The great Windham was in command, and I should say, from his anxiety, he wished himself back in the Redan. Finding out all that had taken place, I rode back and met the C. in Chief coming in, but few of our traps arrived that night, so we had another bivouac, which by the way is far nicer in a novel than in reality, particularly at this time of the year. Since the 12th, I have scarcely seen my tents, and have got a horrid cold, but a young fellow ought not to say much about these things, as the ladies have had to rough it the last few days, many of them being out the whole night. All yesterday, we were employed in crossing the river, and the task will not be finished by this evening I fear—such a string of Hackeries,[1] Elephants, Camels, etc., etc. Our camp is now pitched on the parade of the Dragoons, and my tent is nearly inside the position occupied by Sir H. Wheeler. The Pandies have the City and the Cantonments West of the Assembly Rooms, which place they burnt yesterday destroying property of some 50 or 60 Officers, things that had been left behind on our departure for Lucknow. I like a griff[2] gave a tent to be mended, which I

[1] Indian bullock-carts.

[2] *Griff*, or *Griffin*, an Anglo-Indian name for a new-comer in India.

suppose has gone with the rest. To-morrow our operations will commence, and, if successful, we ought to get all the rebel guns amounting to between 30 and 40 and kill a good many of their 10,000. This will then clear the Doab except Fatehgarh, and that place must be settled shortly, when our dâks will be safe from Peshawur to Calcutta. As it is I received 4 dear letters, my Mother, of the 24th September, a day or two ago, forwarded by some kind friend from Agra; also one from Maria, which I must answer as soon as I can. I wrote to you last mail about a pistol. I have succeeded in getting a very nice one, sold at Mayne's auction, so don't send me any, as I am suited exactly. Colonel Woodford of the Rifle Brigade was shot the day before yesterday here—a friend of Hamilton's I think. The Delhi Despatches have been published. I am mentioned very handsomely, which will, I am sure, please you all, and I hope I shall have the same luck in the Lucknow ones. I fortunately succeeded in one or two affairs Sir Colin picked me out for. The night before the attack, it was found out all the rifle ammunition had been left behind at Alambagh. I was ordered to take 300 camels and a guard of 150 Cavalry and bring all that was available. I started at 8.0 P.M., a horrid dark night, across country, finding my course entirely by the compass, and stars when visible. By daylight in the morning I returned all safe, and went at once to lead the Columns into the City, so that I had a long ride, it being 10 P.M. ere I dismounted again, and under a very heavy fire nearly all the time. Every Officer on the Headquarters staff was either wounded or had his horse shot, except myself and another. If I can write a few lines in this, I will, but for fear of accidents I'll have it ready to send. Some rascals have[1] in our rear and stopped the Calcutta dâk. However, I hope the road will be safe in a day or two. God bless you, my own darling Mother. With my fondest love to the General and dearest Harrie.—Believe me, ever your very affect. son,

FRED. ROBERTS.

1st Dec.—A dâk goes out to-night so I'll send this off. We have been doing nothing all day, but a couple of round shots have just gone over my tent, so I imagine we shall go on now. Good-bye.

FRED. R.

CAMP, CAWNPORE,
Dec. 12th, 1857.

MY DEAREST MOTHER—Since my last letter, we have thrashed the Gwalior troops and taken

[1] Letter torn.

32 guns from them. These, with the 5 they lost before, accounts for nearly the whole of their train, so that much more trouble is not to be expected from those rebels. Fatehgarh now only remains, and at that we go in a few days. Once the Fort there is occupied by our troops, the road from Peshawur to Calcutta will be open for letters and the passage of small detachments of troops. Our success here was very complete, and fortunately with a small loss. We followed the rascals up for 12 miles, cutting up a good many. This gave us so long a trip back to our camp that we had to bivouac for the night, minus dinner, etc., and I like a griff had not even a cloak. However the morning came like other mornings, and affairs settled down. A week has passed since that business, and we are still here waiting for orders to advance. Many things require to be done in these new Regiments, as nearly all have come up without kit of any description, so that our delay here is necessary. The day before our last fight, the 42nd Highlanders joined the Force, besides which we had Detachments from the 2nd and 3rd Batns. Rifle Brigade. It was a magnificent sight, the first advance on the open plain near the Cavalry lines (well remembered I have no doubt by the General), the Artillery were in front, thro' which the enemy's round shot and

shell played sharply, then came bounding over the Infantry drawn up in line, providentially without doing much damage. On we went, and as fast the Pandies retired, leaving their camp in our possession, and making off for their very lives. I have seen battles now in every shape and shall not be sorry to have a rest. Losing so many dear friends and knowing what misery each fight entails is eno' to make one soon satisfied, for a time at any rate. I always longed for service and would not have missed being thro' these past six months for all I hope ever to possess. Few have been lucky eno' to get off so easily as I have. One slight wound. Now, unless we have to return to Oude, our work may be said to be over. I hope to remain at Meerut all the hot weather. The C. in C. will probably be there with a large force. —— was to have joined us, but just before leaving Allahabad he was ordered down to Benares, so I am not likely to see him for some time. Hamilton will, I hope, come up country without delay. At first he must join his Regiment on account of the paucity of Officers, but I see his name is down in Sir Colin's private book for an appointment which he will be sure to get ere long. Norman is now Deputy-Adjutant-General, and the best man in Bengal for the place. We are both very anxious about *Medals*.

One should be given for Delhi alone, and another for other parts of India. The Governor-General[1] does not seem inclined to reward the Army himself, so I hope Parliament will. Fancy having two!!

15*th Dec.*—I have not received anything from you since the 24th Sept., since which 3 Mails have come. All the October letters are, I am afraid, lost for ever, but I hope in a few days now the dâks will travel as usual, and that I shall hear from you again, dearest Mother. I wish I could see you all, were it only for a short time, just to have one or two nice chats. I hope you have sent me out your likenesses by Hamilton. They are taken so easily now that if you have not, *please do so, Mother.* I shall prize them very much, and in return will come home and see you as soon as ever I can!

17*th Dec.*—This must be finished to-day. Wish dear Harriet many happy birthdays from me. I thought of her yesterday, 24 years old. How time flies! On our arrival here from Lucknow, I wrote you a long letter giving an account of all that had taken place there. I hope you received it, tho' at the time it was despatched the road to Calcutta was not very safe. If I am fortunate eno' to be stationed at

[1] Viscount Canning, afterwards Earl Canning, K.G.

Meerut, I shall probably meet Ham. occasionally, which will be very nice, besides it will be a change from Peshawur.

At Allahabad I hear country boats are being got ready to convey all to Calcutta.[1] The Lucknow Despatches have been published. I have now been thanked twice by Government, which may be of use hereafter. Besides these, our fights at Agra and Bulandshahr have to appear in Orders, and they were as hard as any. So Trea Osborne is married again. I am very glad of it and hope her cousin will make her a nice husband. Good-bye, darling Mother. I hope you will all pass a happy Xmas, and that ere many more come round I may be with you. Very kind love to all.—Ever your very affect. son,

FRED. ROBERTS.

CAMP FOUR MARCHES FROM CAWNPORE,
Dec. 28*th*, 1857.

MY DEAREST MOTHER—Here we are nearly at the end of this eventful year. Since my last, dated Cawnpore, little has happened to our particular Force. We were delayed so long for carriage, etc. etc., that we are still three marches from Fatehgarh, and will probably

[1] The women and children who had been brought away from Lucknow.

not arrive there for another week, as Pandy has broken down one or two bridges, which will take some little time to mend. Other Columns have, however, being doing good service. Seton[1] with one from Delhi attacked the rebels near Allyghur on the 19th and captured 15 guns with little or no loss to himself. Outram near Lucknow a few days ago got 4 guns, and, detached from our Force, 2 Brigades are scouring the country between the "Ganges" and "Jumna," they, however, co-operate with us in attacking Fatehgarh, so if Pandy makes a stand, he will probably suffer severely, but I imagine the day before we arrive all will cross quietly over the river and join their friends in Rohilkund and Oude. Our plans are I believe as follows: to go as far as Mainpuri, and there leave a Regiment, which, with a strong detachment at Fatehgarh, will completely open the Trunk road. We then return to Cawnpore and make again for Lucknow. Franks'[2] Force in the Benares district will make a simultaneous movement in the Fyzabad direction, so that by the middle or end of February, the rebels will be, please God, nearly exterminated. What may happen afterwards it is impossible to say. I hoped to have gone

[1] Brigadier T. Seaton, C.B.
[2] General T. H. Franks, C.B.

straight up to Meerut, thinking Oude would have been left to other hands, but the Commander-in-Chief seems determined to go there himself. After all, I had no business to hope anything of the sort. I could not be happier or better than I am now. Garden, of the Quartermaster-General's Department, left for England a few days ago on M.C.[1] Sir Colin was going to put me in his place at once, but Norman very properly suggested that it would be better to wait for Becher's[2] arrival, who is with Seton's Column, before deciding upon anything. It will only occasion a short delay, and no one will be annoyed, for, once I am in the Department permanently, of course they can do as they like. I am greatly pleased at having given Sir Colin satisfaction, for he is rather a particular old gentleman. I am certain of remaining in the Field as long as work has to be done, and most probably with the Headquarters of the Army. My 1st Lieut. dates from June last, which makes my pay Rupees 565 a month, so I hope, darling Mother, to save a little money during the next 2 or 3 years, and then go home to see all you dear ones. Once I get pay for this year, all my debts will be settled, and I shall start 1858 clear!!

[1] Medical Certificate.

[2] Colonel Becher, Quartermaster-General of the Army; afterwards Major-General Sir Arthur Becher, K.C.B.

I was so glad to hear from Hamilton before leaving Cawnpore, and now that we return we are certain of meeting; and may possibly be together for some little time. He will have to join his Regiment I am afraid, all the Officers from Staff are ordered, so they can scarcely let him off. However, I hope it will not be for long. How jolly it will be hearing about you all. I can think of nothing else but seeing old Hamilton. Thank the General very much for his picture. Hamilton tells me it is a very good one. Mother, why don't you and Harriet send me out your likenesses? I won't ask for anything else. Get them taken and direct the box to Grindlay & Co., Calcutta. No letters, my Mother, have come from you since yours of the 24th Sept. I hope, however, in a day or two, all that have collected at Agra will be forwarded on. Poor Gerrard, I am very sorry for his death. Marianne must be in great grief, I have scarcely seen a couple in India so fond of each other as they were.

29th.—We halt here to-day, so I'll finish this altho' I believe a day or two later would be safe. Mackinnon is to be here to-morrow, so I shall hear from him all about "Suir View." I hope dearest Harrie and the General are not suffering from the cold weather. On Xmas Day I drank all your healths in the last bottle of Sherry our Mess contained. There is still a little beer left, after which we must turn to the water system. I have lately directed all letters to you, dearest Mother, as I thought it better for one to have the story of all our fights, etc., and I know you will send my letter to Innes when you think she will be interested. The Despatches about Agra and Bulandshahr have just been published. Mind you read them and tell me what you think. Give my love to the General, Harrie, Innes and John. With the same, my own Mother, to yourself, Believe me, ever your very affect. son,

FRED. ROBERTS.

CAMP NEAR FATEHGARH,
Dec. 31*st*, 1857.

MY DEAREST HARRIET—Altho' I wrote to Mother on the 29th, I must send you a few lines to tell you how jolly and happy I have been the last day or two by coming across Mackinnon, who has given me such a nice account of you all. He seems thoroughly to have enjoyed his visit to Waterford. I am so much obliged to Mother and the General for treating him in the kind way they did. Hearing your names and all your goings on makes me more and more anxious to see you. I wonder when that happy day will come. I can think of nothing else now but meeting Hamilton, and do so long to leave India for a while, and have some quiet days at Suir View. That, however, cannot be yet. If I could keep in health, I would not leave for anything. There must be service for months and months, and your brother Fred, Harriet darling, has no end of ambition, besides soldiers should make up their minds to work with their life's best blood at such a crisis to restore peace and order, and show these rascally Musalmans that, with God's help, Englishmen will still be masters of India. It will be doubly sweet going home when all is over. You must look out for some nice girl with "blue eyes and yellow hair" (such as Mackinnon raves about) for me, Harriet dearest, who will console me for having to return to the gorgeous East. I met Mac. on the evening of the 29th. A Brigade from Cawnpore was coming up to join our Force, and I was sent to halt them 5 or 6 miles in the rear. The first man I saw was Mac. That day year he had been with you. He returned with me and is now living in my tent, so you may fancy how I make him talk about you all.

An order has been sent down to Allahabad

ordering Hamilton to join his Regiment without delay. It is close to us now and will co-operate with us against Fatehgarh, if the rascals make a stand. Hamilton, I am afraid, will scarcely be in time for the scrimmage, but will it not be nice having him with our Force. The 1st Fusiliers join the Commander-in-Chief's camp, and under any circumstances Hamilton must join his Regiment for the present. I have no doubt he will get an appointment ere long, but I hope he will not be disappointed at the Order now sent. He must have expected it fresh from England, but once in the Camp, something will be sure to turn up. While searching over the Nana's Palaces at Bithur the other day, we found heaps of letters directed to that fiend "Azimula Khan"[1] by ladies in England, some from Lady ——, ending "*your affect. Mother.*" Others from a young girl at Brighton named ——, written in the most lovable manner. Such rubbish I never read, partly in French, which this scoundrel seems to have understood; how English ladies can be so infatuated. Miss —— was going to marry Azimula, and I have no doubt would like to still, altho' he was the chief instigator in the Cawnpore massacres. You would not believe

[1] Azimullah Khan was a Mahomedan in the service of the Nana Sahib, whom the latter had employed as his agent in England.

them if I sent home the letters. Next Mail, and I have time, I'll copy one or two out, just to give you an idea of a native rascal's correspondence. —— writes from Benares that he is going to remain there. I hoped he would have joined the Force under Franks and seen some service. He should have tried to have done so. All are, or ought to be, in the field. How are all my old friends Harrie, Miss Dyson, etc. etc.? I like to hear about them. Remember me very kindly to the first. Mind you read all the Despatches. In the Bulandshahr ones I was mentioned by the Cavalry Commanding Officer, also by the Artillery, by the latter for showing the way and being first at the gun we captured!! This will please the General I am sure, and my own darling Mother.

Many thanks for the parcel you have sent me by Mac. All his traps are in Calcutta, but will arrive some day I hope. Good-bye, dearest Harriet. With my fondest love, ever your very affect. brother,

FRED. ROBERTS.

Mackinnon desires to be remembered to all.

CAMP FATEHGARH,
Jan. 12th, 1858.

MY DEAREST FATHER—I have been made so happy by receiving your kind letter of the 23rd October, and one from Mother dated 7th November. Both arrived a day or two after I had despatched my last to you, and, to crown all, Hamilton made his appearance yesterday, looking uncommonly well and jolly. We had such a long chat about Suir View. Hearing of you all makes me long more than ever to go home. At the same time, I would not be away from India now for a great deal. The Fusiliers are so badly off for Officers that Hamilton has no chance of getting away for some time. I wrote and told him this as soon as he landed, and recommended his joining sharp and applying for the Adjutancy. At the same time, I spoke to all I could here about him. I believe he is sure of the appointment. It will give him plenty to do, getting the Regiment set up after all the knocking about it has had, but is the very best thing for him, and one nice part of it is that we shall be together, as the Fusiliers have been put into the 3rd Brigade of Grant's Division. The day after I last wrote (New Year's day), I was ordered with a Brigade to repair the Suspension Bridge over the "Kali Nadi," which had been partially destroyed. A few days previously the rebels were in great force at this place, but, strangely, they retired as we approached and left us unmolested the whole night, so that by the morning of the 2nd, we had the business completed, when back came "Pandy" and opened a couple of guns upon us. We got 2 heavy pieces manned by sailors over, and returned the compliment, and then waited quietly until our troops came all on this side. At 3.0 P.M. we were ready. The Infantry and guns advanced on the village, out of which the rebels were soon driven, and then our Cavalry followed up in two lines led by General Grant. I accompanied the first line, and in the scrimmage captured a very pretty Standard! which I will send home to adorn Suir View the first opportunity. A great piece of luck my getting it, was it not? The evening left 8 guns in our possession, 2 in the village, and 6 were got in the pursuit, besides some 300 dead on the field. Our own loss was trifling. Maxwell of my Regiment received a bad wound in his leg, and one Irregular Cavalry Officer was killed. This success quite took away the rebels' pluck. During the night they deserted the City and station of Fatehgarh, of which we took quiet possession on the 3rd. All the private houses, etc., are completely destroyed, and what must have been a pretty station is now a heap of ruins. A great part of the government wood, however, for gun carriages has been saved, as also a quantity of cloth. These must have been preserved by the Nawab for his own use, and in the hurry of running away were forgotten. The whole of the Doab is now comparatively quiet. At Mainpuri the 38th[1] Queen's are stationed with a couple of guns, and here the 82nd[2] remains with 4 guns, while the 64th[3] Queen's go to Aligarh. This preserves the communication and keeps the rascals to the East of the Ganges. It is still undecided where we are to go to—Lucknow, of course, eventually—but whether thro' Rohilkund or back by Cawnpore depends on circumstances. Outram's Division at Alambagh amounts now to 5000 men, and another Brigade of Infantry is ready formed at Allahabad to join him, if necessary. It will be months and years before the country can be in the state it was before the rebellion, but once our power is firmly re-established, we shall be better than ever. When that time comes, I'll come home and see you. Hamilton has given me such a nice account of Suir View. If we can only get away together, what fun we will have. —— is still at Benares. He complains of bad health. Camp life might

[1] The 1st South Staffordshire Regiment.
[2] The 2nd South Lancashire Regiment.
[3] The 1st North Staffordshire Regiment.

have done him good. At any rate, he should have tried it and accompanied Franks's Column. Opportunities of this sort don't often occur to young men. A name made now will last one's life, and altho' I begin to think Medals will not be given for this service, I have no doubt we shall all be rewarded one way or another. In case you may not see the different Despatches, I enclose you copies of the Orders in which my name is mentioned. This alone rewards me, for I know you and my darling Mother will be pleased to see my name thus publicly brought forward. Becher goes home on medical certificate, his wound has never healed, he asked me for your address, as he intends paying Ireland a visit and would like to see you.

13*th.*—Hamilton has got the Adjutancy, but will have to wait a few days before he can be put in Orders, this is a very nice appointment for him. Becher spoke to him very civilly, and said had he been in the country at the commencement of the mutiny he would have put him into the Department, but that now, of course, others had to be served first, besides which he was required with the Regiment, but that he would remember him.

14*th.*—We changed camp this morning, which looks like remaining here for some time longer. I received yesterday dear Harrie's letter of the 17th Nov. She complains that nothing had been heard of me for some time. I hope, however, that the next Mail will bring news of all my letters having reached you. I wrote constantly: Sept. 15th, Sept. 24th, Oct. 1st, Oct. 14th, Oct. 27th, Dec. 2nd, Dec. 17th, Dec. 29th,[1] giving you accounts of all our doings, and shall be sorry if you do not receive them. On the 19th Hamilton and I dine together to celebrate Mother's birthday. Good-bye. With my kindest love, Believe me ever, my dearest Father, your very affect. son,

FRED. ROBERTS.

HEADQUARTERS CAMP, FATEHGARH,
Jan. 28th, 1858.

MY DEAREST MOTHER—I was made so happy the other day by receiving your dear letter of the 7th December, in which you acknowledge the receipt of all my letters up to the 15th October. How strange that four should have reached you at once. I am glad, however, that they all turned up, otherwise you would have lost part of the story of our goings on, which I try and connect from one letter to

[1] Actual dates of letters: Sept. 16, 26, 30; Oct. 15, 27; Nov. 1, 13, 25; Dec. 12, 28, 31.

another, so that you and the General may understand better than from the Paper what really does happen. Long ere this, you will have heard of my good fortune in having been thro' the Lucknow business. Indeed, I hope next Mail will tell us that you have seen the "Delhi Despatches." We are still at Fatehgarh, but likely ere long to make a move. The rebels don't like coming to close quarters, but hover round us in parties of 2 or 3000, against whom Brigades are constantly sent. One returned yesterday after a very successful business, killing several fanatics and capturing 4 guns. This part of the country has been formed into a District comprising Mainpuri, Elanah, and half way to Cawnpore—all under Colonel Seton—a good Officer, brother of the man in the 1st Fusiliers. Once we leave, master Pandy will, I have no doubt, give some trouble, but he can't do much damage beyond destroying the telegraph wire here and there. After garrisoning all these places, we have still 3 Brigades of Infantry, a large force of Cavalry, 3 troops of H.A. and 2 Batteries, besides some 20 heavy guns and Tombs' Troop of H.A. *en route* from Meerut. Outram has also been considerably increased and Franks is sufficiently strong to protect the country between

Gorruckpore, Azimgarh, and Benares, and in co-operation with Jung Bahadoor's[1] troops will advance on Lucknow from the South East. Pandy must catch it now I think. Hitherto, notwithstanding our great successes, they have never suffered very severely from our paucity of Cavalry. We shall now have "clouds" of horse, one sort and another, who altho' not first rate can follow and cut up the rascals when put to flight, as they invariably are by our guns. Sir Archdale Wilson with his staff arrived in camp a day or two ago for the purpose of commanding all the Artillery in the field. This does not suit our Royal Brethren, who think his appointment a slur on their General (Dupuis) who was ordered back to Calcutta from Cawnpore. Sir Colin is quite right, having a man with him at this crisis who knows about our different Magazines, etc., better than a stranger can possibly do, and if Sir Archdale plays his cards well, our Regiment need not fear of "being absorbed" or left in the background on future occasions. At the same time, I am sorry for the Royal gunners, who are all nice gentlemanly fellows. As Artillerymen, I do not think we need be in

[1] The Prime Minister of Nepal. The Government of India accepted his offer of assistance, and he marched down into India at the head of 10,000 of his Gurkhas.

any alarm of their surpassing us, but unless our field officers are increased and a certain number of 2nd Captains given, they will ever command us. Men of my service are all Captains, so I hope for the best, and expect to be one myself ere long, and then Brevet Major!! When that comes, dearest Mother, I'll come home and pay you a visit. I long to see you all more than ever after hearing from Hamilton such nice accounts of the pleasures and delights of "Home" and England. We had such long chats together and were as happy as possible until the 26th, when an order was issued for the 1st Fusiliers to march to Cawnpore for the purpose of receiving and getting their recruits in order, pending our advance on Lucknow. However, we shall meet again then, please God, and if spared will, I trust, be somewhere near each other next hot weather. Hamilton is just what I expected, a nice, good-looking, jolly fellow. We suit each other admirably. I have just written to him to say that Sir Colin yesterday evening approved of his being appointed Adjutant to his Corps, so he will be in Orders probably before this Mail leaves Calcutta. I tell him that he must not get any stouter. He is quite respectable eno' now for anything. I have not altered in size since I left you in the very least. The clothes I brought out fit me still. Weighing the other day to ride at some races we had in camp, I found I was scarcely 9 stone, yet with this advantage I did not win any, and had a fall in the bargain, so I am still a griff you see, Mother dear.

Thank the General very much for his likeness. *It is perfect.* Just what I wanted and so ridiculously like that I positively can fancy he is speaking to me. Give darling Harriet my very best love for her nice songs. They seem to be very pretty, but I must wait until I see Maggie Boisragon to have them played over to me, as I have not even my flute here. We left the 5th Fusiliers at Alambagh. I will find Meara out whenever I come across the Regiment. So Cusac Smith writes to you still. Remember me to him very kindly, and say when I return home, he must pay Suir View a visit. Nothing is settled yet as to how we advance on Lucknow, whether thro' Rohilkund or *viâ* Cawnpore. After the place is in our possession, a great portion of the troops will, I imagine, go into quarters while the rest must occupy and quiet Bareilly, Moradabad, etc. I should like to be sent with this column, as I have never seen that part of the country, besides I have still a hankering for going North again.

31*st.*—The Order is just out for our march to-morrow back to Cawnpore. The C. in C. goes quickly so as to meet the Governor-General, who will be there. The rest of us go by regular stages, and should reach in a week, so I shall soon see Hamilton again. From Cawnpore, of course, we go at Lucknow, and ere this day month, I hope we may be well inside that horrid city. We shall be so strong in Artillery that I do not anticipate a heavy loss. Master Pandy will be frightened when he finds himself peppered with 68 PRs.! 3 or 4 of which we shall have. Good-bye, dearest Mother. I'll write again from Cawnpore. Give my love to the General, Harrie, Innes, and John.—Ever your very affect. son,

FRED. ROBERTS.

CAMP 10 MILES FROM CAWNPORE,
Feb. 11*th*, 1858.

MY DEAREST MOTHER—Since my last from Fatehgarh, the whole force has marched to Cawnpore, and a great portion have already gone on towards Lucknow. There was some doubt at first to what I should be attached. General Wilson said, being an Artillery Officer

I ought to be on his staff, and General Grant with whom I have been since Delhi, wished to have me with his, the Cavalry Division. Both old fellows have been so kind to me that I thought it prudent not to say anything, but leave matters to chance, which eventually decided that I was to be a Light Dragoon. Were there a likelihood of a long siege, I would prefer the Artillery, but in this business I expect the Cavalry will have the most work, so I am better pleased to be as I am. Pending the junction of all the troops near Lucknow, General Grant has charge of the road from Cawnpore, to see the convoys protected, etc., so we have a roving commission for the present. For the last 3 days, however, we have been here (Unao) with the 1st Fusiliers, so I have had the pleasure of dear Hamilton's society. To-morrow we move a few miles nearer to Alambagh, and by the 20th I hope the whole force will be assembled at Lucknow with our Army. The business cannot be a very long one. Sir Colin has under him:

1st. The Artillery Division, consisting of 2 Brigades, Field and Siege Artillery, 54 guns of the former and 65 of the latter, all well manned and provided with ammunition.

2nd. Engineer Brigade. Two Companies of Royal and nearly 1000 Native Sappers.

3rd. The Cavalry Division, a very fair one mustering about 4000 sabres.

4th. Three Divisions of Infantry, comprising 15 European and 3 Native Regiments—nearly 20,000 men. All healthy and sound.

Six of the heavy guns are 68 PRs. worked by sailors, which will astonish the Natives. Ten days should see us in possession of Lucknow. Then will come the tedious work of dispersing the various bands of rascals that will be scattered all over Oude. Almost a hopeless business, unless some of the chief men come over to our side and listen to reason. I sincerely hope there will be no occasion to spend another hot weather in tents. I shall have had eno' knocking about when Lucknow has fallen, and would like then to be stationed somewhere about Meerut or Umballa, until my time is up to go home. I look forward to that now more than ever. Four years, however, must pass, unless I can get sick leave. This Order about prize money, however, renders me quite independent, as my share as a Captain will be at least £400 or £500, it may be a great deal more, so that

I shall have something to spend on furlo', and if I have to wait 4 years, I may hope to have as much more of my own. Tell the General that in March or April I am going to send him £100 to be put into the 7 per cent loan Hamilton informs me he has opened! This will just be a commencement to show the dear General that there is still some hope for me. My own Mother, I have such a piece of news for you. I have been recommended for the "*Victoria Cross.*" The letter says for "repeated gallantry in the field, more especially on the 2nd Jan. 1858, when Lieut. Fred. Roberts captured a rebel standard, killing the Standard Bearer, and on the same day saved the life of an Irregular Cavalryman by cutting down a Sepoy who was attacking him with a musket and Bayonet." Is not this glorious? How pleased it will make the General. *Such a Medal* to wear with "*For Valour*" scrolled on it. How proud I shall be, darling Mother, when I show it to you—better than all the other Medals put together. All get Medals when given for a campaign, but few, very few, this glorious Cross. The papers go before Sir Colin to-day, so ere I close this I shall know for certain whether I am to get it or not. My name has also gone in for a Brevet Majority on promotion to a Company. Major Fred. Roberts, V.C.! will sound well, will it not? All this before our grand smash at Lucknow too. If I could only get the Majority *now*,[1] but that is impossible, and I may be, unless great alterations in the Regiment are made, 8½ years more a Subaltern. However, then I must be a Brevet Captain which would give me the Majority, but we'll hope for better luck than that. All has prospered with me as yet. Few young fellows in the Army have been so lucky, and I always look forward to everything turning out well. I want Hamilton now to get V.C. and Brevet Majority, then all will be right. —— I am afraid will get neither as long as he remains out of the field, but, of course, if sick, he can't help himself, yet the strange part of this campaign has been to show how wonderfully well men who have been proverbially sick and delicate have kept their health, and fared even better than their neighbours, so I wish —— had tried the receipt.

At Cawnpore I met and breakfasted with Hallett Batten. He is an eccentric fellow, but very amusing. He reminded me more of his sister Priscilla than any of the others—the same way of speaking and shaking his head. Hamilton's Regiment is brigaded with the 23rd Fusiliers[2] and 79th Highlanders.[2] He likes

[1] He got his brevet majority in 1860.

[2] The Royal Welch Fusiliers and the Cameron Highlanders.

this, as he knows the latter Corps well. I do not expect any great opposition. We are too strong for that, so you must not be very anxious, my own darling Mother, about Hamilton and me. Very different fighting from what we have hitherto had. No anxiety like Delhi. In fact, we are doing things in a gentlemanly way, and all will soon be over. By the 1st March, we should be dining quietly in Lucknow, arranging for the housing of a good strong garrison and for detaching the remainder in various directions. I had such a nice letter from Annie Thompson[1] a day or two ago, written on the 19th December, giving me a long account of you all. She is a dear little body, and I am very glad you like her. At Simla both George and Annie were very kind to me. No letters have come from you by the 26th Dec. Mail as yet, but I hope to receive some to-day or to-morrow. Good-bye, my fondly loved Mother. Very kind love to the General, Harrie, Innes, John, etc.—Ever your very affect. son,

FRED. ROBERTS.

Hamilton sends his love. He will write shortly.

[1] A cousin.

CAMP "BUNNEE,"
Feb. 13.

I had hoped that by to-day I should have been able to give you some certain information about the V.C., but it seems that the business cannot be decided just yet. Norman writes: "The Chief will, I think, give you the Victoria Cross, but the papers will have to be submitted again with some others. However, I think you may be quite easy as to obtaining it, tho' not for some little time." This looks as if it were all right—only delayed by official routine. However, I shall be very anxious until I see my name in General Orders. I came on here yesterday, leaving Hamilton's Regiment about 10 miles behind, and here I am likely to remain for some days, close to the place where poor Mayne and I last November were so nearly cut off while marking out the camp—*experientia docet*, and I am not likely to be caught in a trap again. No letters from you as yet, Mother, tho' the mail of the 26th Dec. *viâ* Lahore and Delhi has been in for some days. Mine have, I suppose, been delayed at one place or another and will turn up eventually. Good-bye again, darling Mother.—Your affect. son,

FRED. ROBERTS.

CAMP NEAR LUCKNOW,
Feb. 26th, 1858.

MY DEAREST HARRIET—A day or two after sending off my last letter, Orders came for General Grant to proceed with a force into the District towards the North of the Lucknow and Cawnpore Road, for the purpose of driving away various bands of rebels who had collected there, and who it was feared would annoy our communication while passing convoys, etc., backwards and forwards, so we had to start off again. On the way, I managed to spend one day with Hamilton, who was very much disgusted at his Corps being left behind, but all, of course, could not come. We at first took a course nearly parallel to the Ganges, and one day were only 20 miles from where the Nana Sahib was hiding. This was a sad temptation to go on, but Sir Colin, for fear of our being led away too far had given orders we were not to proceed beyond a certain place, so we were obliged to leave the fiend for some other day and turn our steps towards Lucknow. Day after day the enemy fell back before us, until the 23rd, when thinking themselves tolerably secure inside a strongly walled village, they held out. We first of all came across their Cavalry, who as usual bolted as we gradually approached, seeking protection from the fire from the village, which opened upon us as we came in sight. The gates were all strongly barricaded, so it was necessary to make a breach. This our heavy guns soon effected, when in went the Infantry clearing the place out in fine style. Our Cavalry were on the look out and cut up some 400 of the rascals as they came flying out. The success was complete. We only had 20 casualties, took six guns of sorts and killed upwards of 500. Yesterday, the 25th, we halted for the purpose of destroying the place, which was done most effectually. It makes one very sad, however, dearest Harriet, in the midst of all our success to see what distress a small fight of this kind even occasions. I went into the village last evening to see what damage was being done to the defences. Nearly all the houses had been burnt, except in one corner. As I approached, a very old man met me and said "here are two cows; I have still another in the house, which I will bring out to you, but for God's sake don't burn the only property I have in the world. Yesterday morning I had five sons. See, here are three of them, the other two fled away, and I don't know whether they have shared the same fate and are dead, or whether they may have escaped. None of us ever bore arms against your Government. We are all labourers. Ever since the rebellion took place, I have prayed for your success, and if all my sons are killed, I shall still pray for you, for I know under any other rule we have nothing but oppression and tyranny to expect." The old man went on for a long time and seemed so truthful that I had not the heart to burn his house. Going a little farther, I came on three women watching the dead bodies of their husbands, none of them Sepoys I believe. It was such a sad sight, however, that I felt quite unhappy and wished most sincerely this horrid war was at an end. You must not think, darling Harriet, that I pity the Sepoys or black-guards who are rebelling against us. On the contrary, few are more unrelenting than I am. When a prisoner is brought in, I am the first to call out to have him hanged, knowing that unless the severest measures are adopted we shall have no end to our war, but it does make one melancholy to come across accidents such as I have related. They cannot be avoided I well know. Soldiers get into a town, and cannot be expected to distinguish between the guilty and innocent in the heat of the moment, yet such scenes make one wish that all was settled. Like everything else, one can have eno' of fighting I suppose. It would never do to leave Lucknow. That must be completely

Emery Walker ph. sc.

Harriet Roberts (aet. 21)

From a pastel drawing by E. Grimston

smashed. Afterwards, we can afford to rest and call on the head men in Oude to make terms, it will be the quickest way of getting rid of the Sepoys, as they will gradually be given up. Were we to fight for ten years we should never kill half of them. Your dear letter of the 24th December I received a few days ago. It made me so happy, darling Harriet. You write so nice and kindly that I love you more, if possible, every time I hear from you. Thank the General very much for the pistols he has sent out. I shall prize them above all things. I wrote once and said that I did not care for them, having purchased a new revolver, but I find that revolvers are of little use. On the 23rd I had occasion for a pistol, and was very nearly played a trick by my new one, which I will part with as soon as the double-barrelled arrive. I have written to Allen & Deffell about forwarding them on. Nothing has been settled yet about the "Victoria Cross," at least my name has not been in orders, tho' I believe Sir Colin fully intends me to get it. You may perhaps see the *Gazette* before I do. I should like you also to see my Medal, and will try and see if that can be managed by having it sent thro' you. Such a long time has elapsed since Delhi fell that I do not think they intend giving a Medal for it, but perhaps one for the whole war at the end of the campaign, with Clasps. Well, I don't care so much now having got the V.C., which is worth all the others. I would like the Brevet Majority, but don't see how that can be managed, and I may remain a Subaltern for many a long year—not likely if they put our Regiment on a footing with the Royal Artillery—that would promote me at once!! I'll find out Meara as soon as we reach Alambagh. Hamilton, I imagine, is there before me. A native I sent with a letter to him yesterday has just returned with the news that the 1st Fusiliers had marched in the Lucknow direction. We are only one march off now, and may go on to-morrow, so I'll soon meet old Hamilton again. It is great pleasure being with him—such a nice jolly fellow he is. You can't think, dearest Harrie, how I long and long to see you all. I think of nothing else but going home, and am saving as fast as I can so as to have a little money to go about with, for Major Fred. Roberts, V.C., must cut a dash you know, Harriet. However, I can always get prize money advanced at a slight discount, so that if I get in the least sick, I'll be off this year. Another hot season in tents would, I feel, knock me up. This constant exposure tells, and I already feel hardly up to any great fatigue. We may get into quarters after Lucknow, but more likely not to I think, at least part of us, and I am vain eno' to hope that if a force is sent anywhere, I may be selected for it. After all my preaching about the war being over, Harriet, you will laugh at my wishing to go on. I do wish the war over, but at the same time, I hope I may be actively employed until it is finished, hot weather or cold.

26*th.*—Last night I received a long letter from dearest Innes, the same date as yours. I was very glad to hear from her and will answer her if I can this Mail. We moved our camp across a small river this morning, and are looking out for an attack. I doubt much, however, Pandy making up his mind to come on. A large force started from Lucknow yesterday for the purpose of *destroying* us, but they halted 9 miles off and are there still. If they would only come we should give them such a thrashing, having a nice open country all round.

28*th.*—I must finish this to-day and send it into Cawnpore. My letters take so long *viâ* Lahore, and as I have no chance of seeing the Punjab again for some little time, the best plan will be to direct to Calcutta to the care of "Grindlay & Co." They always know my address. Hamilton writes from Alambagh that he has received letters of the 7th Jan. and mine will not be here for 10 days more probably, so send that way please dearest. Norman writes that the Commander-in-Chief is to be at Bunnee on the 1st, when a general advance is to be made on Lucknow. I don't know whether we join him there, or go direct to Alambagh. Once the business commences we should have Lucknow in our possession in a fortnight, so that by the 15th prox. all will I hope be over. I am having some very smart collars made, like Hamilton's, those that turn over. They suit my large beard famously. Now I never wear any. I sent one of Hamilton's to Maggie Boisragon, and she is having them made for me. Good-bye, dear darling Harriet. Give my fondest love to the General, Mother, Innes and John, and accept the same from your very affect. brother,

FRED. ROBERTS.

CAMP, LUCKNOW,
March 12th, 1858.

MY DEAREST FATHER—I think I had better write you a few lines to-night to thank you for your kind, long letter of the 30th Dec. which I duly received, as in these times it is difficult to know when one may be able to write, and the Mail leaves, I believe, in a few days. We are getting on here slowly, tho' securely. Sir Colin's first act, after taking the Dilkusha was to throw a bridge over the Gumti, and cross over the greater part of the Cavalry and Horse Artillery, and one Division of Infantry, the whole under the Command of General Outram. I, of course, accompanied the Cavalry, and as Hamilton's Corps happened to be in the 3rd Division, we have been together the whole time. The movement was most successful, for besides cutting off all the supplies which were drawn from this part of the country, we have been able to enfilade the line of works the rebels had erected on the line of the Canal—a most formidable position and one that would have cost many valuable lives but for the great error they made in not erecting a flanking defence on this bank. With a little trouble, we were able to see completely in rear of their batteries, and thus prevented their firing a shot—from a fortification which must have taken them weeks to make—perfect in every way but for this one grand mistake. While Sir Colin advanced on the right bank, we quietly took up our position on the left. Yesterday, however, both had difficult work to perform. Sir Colin wished us to gain the Iron

Bridge while he stormed the Begum's Palace. Both operations were carried out with a loss to our forces of some 150 killed and wounded. The enemy must have suffered very severely. In one pit upwards of 500 bodies were thrown —nearly all Sepoys. We had the easiest task owing to their not expecting us. Our loss was 3 Officers killed—2 in the Rifle Brigade, and 1 in the Quartermaster-General's Department, and some 50 or 60 men killed and wounded. The remainder fell on the other side.[1] Amongst the latter was Hodson whom you must remember at Peshawur, a gallant soldier. He died this morning and is a sad loss. His death was entirely owing to himself. He should have been at the time miles away with his own Regiment, but a strange fatality urged him on I suppose.[2] We manage now to hem in Pandy pretty well on all sides. Individuals can escape, but supplies are completely cut off. This disheartens them more than anything. Many run away every night, some make for Bareilly, but the chief part go to their homes, hoping their lives may be spared. The She-Devil of a Begum is still inside inciting the Sepoys to fight to the last. Her traps are, however, all packed ready for a start,

[1] In Sir Colin Campbell's Force on the right bank.

[2] See footnote, p. 225, one-volume edition, of *Forty-One Years in India*, which gives the correct account of this episode.

and I doubt not but that she will be off in a day or two. It is just possible I may be able to send you a line by this Mail to announce the fall of Lucknow, as there is still a day or two to spare, but I think you will have to wait for the next steamer ere the business can be settled. The City is an enormous place, and there are some who will, of course, fight to the very last. I trust they may, and that we may get their guns, otherwise it will entail trouble hereafter. A Column will have to follow up in the Rohilkund direction and see the last under any circumstances. I fancy I shall go with it, tho' I am nearly tired of fighting and shall not be sorry to be quiet. The weather is getting hot now, at least a little too hot for pleasure, tho' not unhealthy. This last *Gazette* promoting all the Delhi heroes bothers some of us Subalterns amazingly. I am the only man in the Quartermaster-General's Department who has had the good fortune to be thro' all, and am the only one who has not got a Brevet. It can't be helped, I know, under the present rule, but it seems rather absurd. Dear old Norman is in the same fix, and as they cannot possibly pass him over until he becomes a Captain I hope they will make one or two more exceptions. It would be a great thing for me getting a Majority now, and really of little use 6 or 7 years hence. Few young fellows have had the luck to see so much hard service as I have, and I can't help thinking the reward will come ere long. A Punjab Battery fell vacant the other day, so I wrote to Norman to know whether I should apply for it. He said: "apply for it by all means. It can do no harm and may do good, but don't be anxious about the result. Happen what may, you are all right—thanks to yourself"; so that if I do not get this appointment, I am safe for something worth having. The only hitch in the Punjab Batteries is my being junior in the Artillery to existing 2nd in Commands. However, I intend to wait patiently and hope that something will turn up. Sir Colin, I know, wishes me well. Talking to me the other day rather warmly about Staff Officers rushing on ahead, he said, seeing a smile on my face: "I am in earnest. Were it my best friend, or one of the best Staff Officers in India (and as such I consider you, my dear Roberts) I would send him back to his Regiment, if I caught him out of his place." I happened to answer him properly, and left him in high favour. So, my dear old Father, your idle son after all the trouble he has cost you may yet do you honour, and prove that all the money and trouble you have spent on him has not been thrown away. I only wish I could go home and see you, if only for a few months. When you were in India, I was young and giddy. I am different now, and if I live, hope to be a General, K.C.B., and all sorts of things. Tired as I am of fighting now, I would not be [in] any other profession for a Kingdom, whether as Infantry, Cavalry, Artillery or Engineers. I have seen all and tried all, and I scarcely know which branch to choose. The Artillery perhaps is my favourite. It is indeed a noble service. So, you have the satisfaction to think that whatever has happened, I am in the very berth I like best. I can never be too thankful to you for all you have done for me. Whatever success I may achieve belongs entirely to you and my own Mother. You have been goodness itself to me, and I know that but for your love and kindness I should never be in my present position. Tell darling Harriet her letter of the 18th January arrived yesterday. I have not found Meara out yet. He is quartered at Alambagh, some 7 miles from this, and my time is too much taken up during the day to ride so far. I will, however, make his acquaintance the very first opportunity. Dear old Hamilton is, however, a far better hand than I am in finding people out. I don't care about knowing many, and require to be well acquainted before I become friends. A few suit me best. Franks' Force arrived the other day and yesterday Jung

Bahadur with some 9000 Ghoorkas made his appearance. What a pity —— did not accompany Franks. He would have been with us now instead of kicking his heels at Benares, besides the march might have done him good. I only hope I may not meet him very soon, for I should certainly tell him that he had no business to remain behind under any circumstances. Writing is too much trouble, so he is not likely to hear unless we come across each other, and that does not seem likely. We heard a day or two ago of the wreck of the *Asa.* Poor Lady Inglis, after all her troubles at Lucknow, being so near death again was very sad. The mails were lost, which is a nuisance. I wrote a long letter to mother from Fatehgarh, as also did Hamilton from Cawnpore. I wrote besides to Mrs. Tom. Tell her so, please, as I have not time to write again this mail. I am never in my tent except at night, and am so sleepy then that I can scarcely scribble at all. Very often the General sleeps at some Picquet, very properly to see that all is right. I, of course, accompany him, and don't much care now whether I am in bed or on the ground. During the cold weather it was different, sleeping out at night was anything but pleasant.

13*th March.*—Not much doing to-day,

beyond extending our position by the Ghoorka Force occupying the line of the Canal towards Alambagh. One more house has to be taken before our Batteries can be got into a good position for breaching the "Kaisarbagh." This will probably be effected to-morrow, and then 24 hours' banging should open the way for our troops. By the 18th all will, I think, be over. Once the Kaisarbagh is ours, Pandy will not remain. I will answer all your questions about the origin, etc., of the mutiny in my next. This letter is long eno'. You must get Harriet to read it. My ink, from the dust, has become pea soup, and the wind (nearly a hot blast) has split all the pens. Good-bye, my dearest Father. With fond love to Mother, Harrie, Innes and John, ever your very affect. son,

FRED. ROBERTS.

CAMP LUCKNOW,
Mar. 15th, 1858.

MY DEAREST MOTHER—This will, I think, be in time for the mail, and tho' but a few lines, will, I know, be very acceptable to you, when you hear that Lucknow is ours, and that both Hamilton and I are well and "jolly." The rebels found we were gradually surrounding them, so for fear of being hemmed in, they suddenly deserted and never fired a shot from their stronghold, the "Kaisarbagh." This has saved us many a gallant fellow's life, and an infinity of trouble. An Order has just come for the H.A. and Cavalry to get ready for a start. Our destination, I believe, is "Sitapur," some 50 miles off. We shall then return here and join a Column bound for Rohilkund. It is rather a nuisance starting off in such a hurry, without even seeing the inside of the place, but I suppose it can't be helped. The Infantry all remain behind, so you will have an account from Hamilton about the Palaces, captured ladies, etc. The war may now fairly be thought over. Occasional scrimmages will probably take place, but there is no fear of any number collecting together again. Just finished in very good time. It is getting too hot for pleasure knocking about all day. It will be a couple of months yet perhaps before some of us find ourselves in houses, but as long as you have not to serve in Batteries, or patrol miles and miles during the heat of the day; mere marching does not do much harm in April and May. I left Peshawur on the 14th of last May, so I shall just have a year of it. My own Mother, if I could only get home now to see you, how truly happy I should be, more especially if I get the Brevet Majority.

Norman seems to think that a few Subalterns will be made, and that I have as good a chance as any. I shall be indeed a lucky fellow—a Major at 25, with the "Victoria Cross," and sure of a good appointment, it would be perhaps better to remain for a few months longer just to get something before things settle down, strike while the iron's hot, and then try for a Medical Certificate and spend 15 months with you dear ones. Were I to leave now they might forget Fred. Roberts. Not likely, however, to do so as long as I am with them. A very nice fellow named Probyn[1] goes home immediately, we have been together the whole time, he is now quite knocked up from the work and exposure. I have given him the Standard which he is to take to you himself. He is such a fine, handsome fellow, I am sure you will like him. The woodwork of the Standard I have not sent, it would take up too much room, Probyn will, however, have it made up for you. He will tell you all that has happened, all about our many fights. Indeed, as I cannot go myself, I could not send a better person to give you an account of this eventful year. Good-bye, my fondly loved Mother. With love to all, ever your affect. son,

FRED. ROBERTS.

[1] Now General Sir Dighton Probyn, V.C., G.C.B.

CAMP NEAR LUCKNOW,
Mar. 27th, 1858.

MY DEAREST MOTHER—I think I shall be in time for the mail that leaves Bombay on the 9th prox., so I'll write you a few lines to-day, as I have no doubt, my Mother, that you are all very anxious about Hamilton and me, and would be glad of news every day. When I wrote to you on the 15th, I was under orders for a move the following day to "Sitapur," and expected that our Column would then proceed to Bareilly. However, Sir Colin found that, altho' the greater part of Lucknow was in our possession, in a few places the rebels were still holding out, so our start was countermanded and now we are waiting for the decision of the Governor-General as to what strength our force is to be, and in what direction we should go first. The sooner he makes up his mind the better. April will soon be here and some of the Regiments have to march back as far as Umballa, which station they cannot possibly reach before the middle or end of May. I left Peshawur on the 14th of last May, and I expect it will be just a year ere I get into a house again. I am only afraid of getting knocked up. I have been more or less seedy the last few weeks, and am now suffering from a slight attack of liver and fever. Nothing very serious, but if I am troubled much I'll be off home. I would like to remain until all is settled, and then get a sick certificate, but at the same time, I would not run the risk of a campaign at this season unless quite well. On the 22nd we were sent about 16 miles off to disperse some rebels who had assembled with 14 guns. Our success was great. The villagers in the neighbourhood gave such good information that I was able to lead the Column on the flank of the rascals as they were making off. Consequently, we captured all their guns and killed several, with the loss, however, of two very dear friends of mine; Macdonnell of the 2nd Punjab Cavalry, such a fine gallant fellow, killed by a bullet thro' his head, was one. I picked him up almost immediately after he fell. He was quite insensible and died in a few seconds. I could scarcely check a tear when I saw the poor fellow I had been laughing with a few moments before lying dead. It makes one horribly tired of fighting, these sad sights, Mother. . . . We have lost 66 Officers altogether at Lucknow this time, smaller perhaps than we should have expected, but eno' to sicken one. In case Meara should not write you can tell his friends he is all well. I have not seen him yet, but will try and do so before we leave. His Regiment, I imagine, remains in Garrison here. Some 8 or 10 Corps are to stay, but none are told off, owing to the Governor-General not making up his mind. Hamilton I saw a day or two ago looking very jolly. He gets on capitally as Adjutant, and for the present I tell him he must be satisfied. Eventually, I have no doubt Sir Colin and Norman will get him a good appointment, but their first object is to get the Fusiliers into order after all the knocking about they have had. Old Hamilton won't quite see this, but as I tell him, it will be all right in the end. Mackinnon is with us here. He sends his kind regards. When we do start, the Brigade Hamilton belongs to is, I think, sure of accompanying our Column, as also Mackinnon's troop, so we shall be together, which is very nice.

28*th.*—I must finish this to-day. I can't help thinking that you will see me ere very long, Mother. My side has been so painful all night that I have been ordered 40 leeches. This may perhaps cure me, but if I still feel ill, you may be sure I'll be off. I am under the care of a first-rate Doctor named Maxwell, so you need not be anxious about me, darling Mother, as there is after all nothing very serious the matter. Maxwell said something last night about the Hills, but I have made up my mind to go home, if I am obliged to leave the field. Only a fair reward I think after all the recent hard work. You shall hear next mail whether I am to be off or not. It makes me almost wild to think how very happy seeing you all will make me. I have written a note to Hamilton to ask him if he can spare an hour or two to ride over and have a chat with me, so I'll keep this open to see if he comes. With kind love to all, believe me, ever your very affect. son,

FRED. ROBERTS.

Tell the General I have sent him home £100 thro' Grindlay!!—F. R.

LUCKNOW,
April 2nd, 1858.

MY DEAREST MOTHER—I hope these few lines will be in time for the mail of the 9th from Calcutta. I write to tell you that I have passed the Committee, and leave shortly for old England on 15 months' leave. I am too weak to travel just yet, so will not be able to start by the 23rd April steamer. I hope, however, to get off by the first one in May. Another reason for my not being anxious to start sooner is that a vacancy has just occurred in the Quartermaster-General's Department, for which the Chief has sent up my name. If I leave this before I am in orders, I lose nearly £100 (half staff for six months) which I can scarcely afford to do. The answer is only a matter of some days, and I shall make for Cawnpore, probably about the 12th. I am in a good house here, and have every care taken of me, so could not be better off. Dear Hamilton can't come with me I am sorry to say, his Regiment has gone to Camp, but what the result is to be no one knows. It is getting too hot now for work. I'll write a long letter next Mail. Write a short answer to the Post Office at Alexandria—it may find me. God bless you all. With love, your affect. son,

FRED. ROBERTS.

I'll go by Trieste or Marseilles.—F. R.

LUCKNOW,
April 10th, 1858.

MY DEAREST MOTHER—I wrote you a few lines on the 2nd *viâ* Calcutta, the day I passed the Committee for 15 months' leave to England. You will probably receive this about the same time, but as I am now able to tell you all my plans, I must have another chat. At first I thought of going thro' the Continent, *viâ* Trieste, but it struck me that this might delay me longer than I wished, so I decided on taking my passage direct to Marseilles, which I have done in the steamer that leaves Calcutta on the 5th May. This takes me to Alexandria by the 3rd June, Marseilles about the 13th or 14th, and to London by the 16th or 17th. I shall stop there one week to fit myself out and get my traps, which will come round by Southampton, then get into the train, go to dear Innes' for a couple of days, thence to Milford, and be with you, my own darling Mother, on the 27th or 28th June. I can scarcely believe that I shall see you so soon. This last week I have improved wonderfully from the thoughts of being with you again. I am, however, done up, and perfectly unfit for work. Were it not so, I would almost prefer remaining in India another year before I took leave. I should then have more money to spend. As it is now I have not much spare cash, but I think I should be doing wrong to stay now, besides I can borrow money on security of my share in the prize property, which will come to £500 they say. I have made up my mind to enjoy myself thoroughly, go everywhere and see everything, which, in England, cannot be done for nothing, and as I always meant my prize money for this purpose, I must try and borrow £300, which will do me famously, and which I shall be able to pay off again without involving myself. So, after all, I have nothing to regret. I am going to write to John Taylor by this Mail to see about having me made a member of the Club, if I am not one already, and to take Hamilton's old lodging for one week for me. You will receive this in time to send a letter to meet me at Marseilles. I will call at the Post Office there, also give a letter to Taylor for me, as I shall be so anxious to hear from you, Mother. The mails now seem to go all wrong. I have not had a line from any of you since the 17th January, and papers have been received from London as late as the 2nd March. The fact is, Bombay is the only way to direct now, owing to the new arrangement about steamers. I leave this to-morrow with the Headquarters' Camp and march in 4 days to Cawnpore. By that time, I shall certainly have an answer about my appointment to the Quartermaster-General's Department, and will then start off dâk for Calcutta, stay a day or two at Allahabad and Benares. I ought to meet George Thompson on the road somewhere unless he returns by Bombay. I saw his name once in the papers as coming out, but have not remarked his arrival. Hamilton is writing himself, so will give you all the news. His Corps stays here for the present, probably for the hot weather. My old Chief, Grant, commands at Lucknow. Sir Colin will, I fancy, go to Rohilkund. Good-bye, dearest Mother. If I am able, you shall hear from me once again ere I start. With fond love to all, believe me, ever your very affect. son,

FRED. ROBERTS.

I enclose the 2nd Bill of Exchange, in case the General may not have received the first forwarded by Grindlay direct.—F. R.

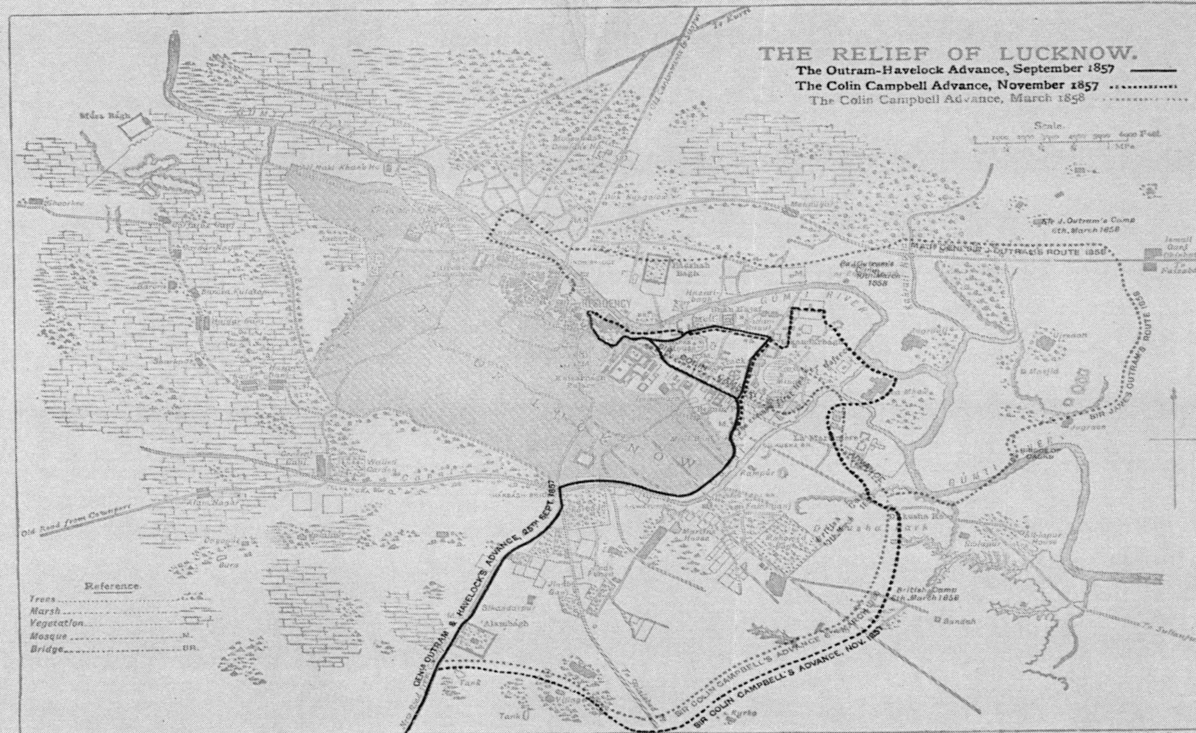
THE RELIEF OF LUCKNOW.
The Outram-Havelock Advance, September 1857
The Colin Campbell Advance, November 1857
The Colin Campbell Advance, March 1858
Scale.
Reference
Trees
Marsh
Vegetation
Mosque
Bridge
GUMTI RIVER
RESIDENCY
GENL OUTRAM & HAVELOCK'S ADVANCE, 25TH SEPT. 1857
SIR COLIN CAMPBELL'S ADVANCE, NOV. 1857
SIR JAMES OUTRAM'S ROUTE 1858
Sir J. Outram's Camp 6th. March 1858
British Camp 5th. March 1858
Alambagh
Old Road from Cawnpore
To Sultanpur
Walker & Boutall sc.

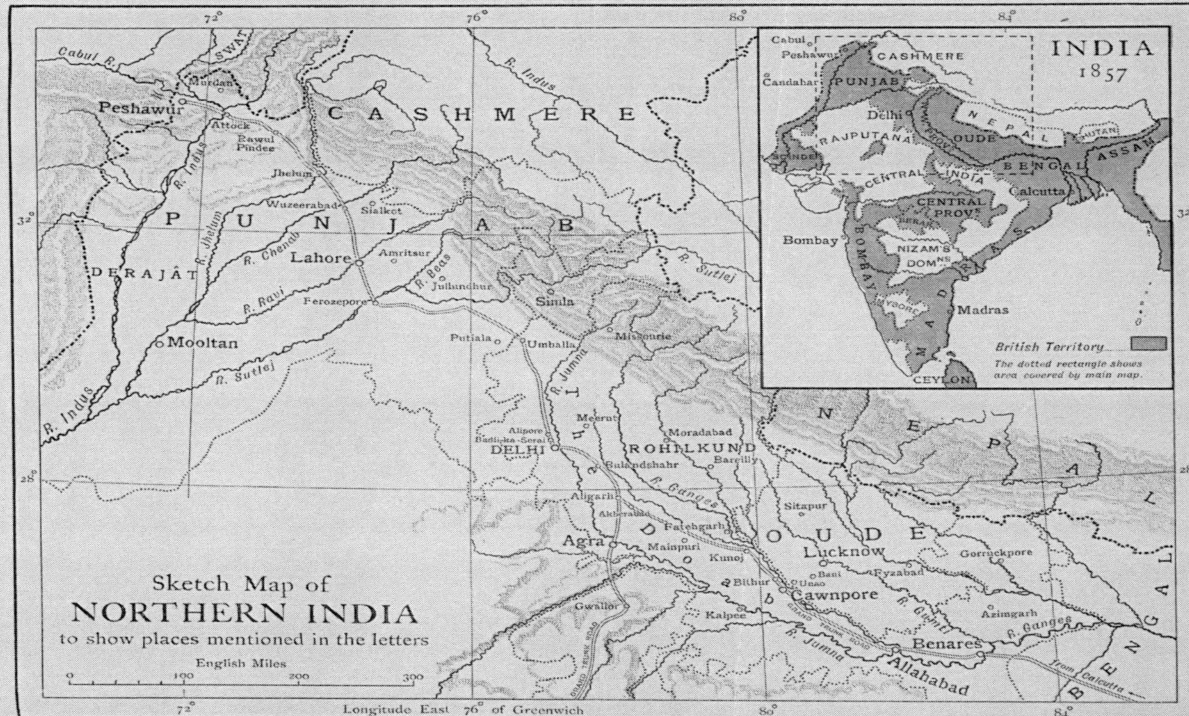

Sketch Map of
NORTHERN INDIA
to show places mentioned in the letters

APPENDIX

To Colonel Becher,
Quartermaster-General of the Army.

Camp Agra,
October 12th, 1857.

Sir—I have the honor to report for your information the following movements of the Moveable Column detached from the Delhi Field Force, since the 8th instant. On that day we were encamped at Bhijghur, about 14 miles from Allyghur, and on account of several letters coming from the Chief Commissioner at Agra, announcing the approach of the rebel troops from the Fort of Dholepore, Colonel Greathed determined on sending the Cavalry and Horse Artillery part of the Column on to Agra as fast as practicable—that night we marched to "Saidabad" *viâ* "Hattrass"—leaving the Infantry halted at the latter place. Soon after reaching "Saidabad," an express came desiring us to proceed at once to "Kundowlee." We bivouacked there for a few hours until joined by the Infantry under Colonel Greathed, when the whole Column marched on Agra, arriving there at daybreak on the 10th inst., thus accomplishing a distance of 45 miles in 30 hours. We were directed to encamp on the Brigade Parade ground, about 2 miles from the Fort in the Gwalior direction. I marked out the ground and then proceeded to make enquiries regarding the movements of the enemy.

The several Civil and Military Authorities in the Fort informed me that from the latest intelligence they had received, there was no doubt but that the rebel Troops having heard of our arrival were in full retreat, and had crossed the "Kharee" Nuddee some 11 miles from the Fort towards Gwalior. From the length of the march but little Baggage came up with the Troops, a few tents had, however, been pitched, when about 9 A.M. a round shot from a heavy gun came right thro' our Camp, this was speedily followed by more, and a heavy cannonade took place. From being so completely surprised, at first there was a slight confusion, however, the Artillery soon brought their guns to bear on the Enemy's Battery, and our Cavalry and Infantry formed up in support. The Irregulars on the right and the 9th Lancers on the left, with 50 of Hodson's Horse in advance. From the high cultivation all round it was difficult to tell on what point the Enemy intended to attack, as we could see nothing but the smoke of their guns. This was, however, speedily settled, as their Cavalry to the amount of some 600 or 700 gallopped round our left, driving Hodson's Horse before them, and making their way straight for our rear. One of the H.A. guns, of which two horses had been killed, was slightly detached from the remainder of the Troop. This was immediately surrounded by the Enemy's Cavalry, the gunners were all cut down, and for a few minutes it was in the possession of the

Enemy. A charge from a squadron of the 9th Lancers, assisted by a well directed fire from the 2nd Punjab Infantry, then in square, speedily effected its recapture. The 9th Lancers then charged the main body of the Cavalry, who dispersed, except a few, and these were all disposed of very prettily in single combats. About this time one of the enemy's waggons blew up, and our Irregular Cavalry returned from the right, where they had been busily engaged with, and completely driven back with great slaughter, large numbers of the Enemy's Cavalry. We advanced the whole line and came upon two heavy brass guns, which had been deserted, up went another ammunition waggon, and from this time the rebels scarcely made a stand. The 3rd Europeans from the Fort had joined the Force, as also the Battery, and it was determined to follow up our success by pursuing as far as possible. On we went to the banks of the "Nuddee," cutting up several on the road, capturing *12 guns* and all their Hackeries. About the 5th mile we passed the Enemy's Camp, which had evidently been pitched for some time, and from the width and depth of the stream, and the enormous size of some of their guns—(large brass 18 PRs. and 24 PRs.)—it is quite impossible they could have been less than two days in crossing all over, so that it is difficult to say how we were allowed to be so surprised. 600 or 700 of the enemy at the least were slain, our casualties amounted to some 60. Ere we reached Camp, the greater part of the Force had travelled 66 miles in 40 hours, and fought a severe action. Part of the way the Europeans were carried on elephants, but the 2 regiments of

Punjab Infantry marched the whole distance, and shewed no signs of fatigue.

I believe we are intended to halt here, until joined by the reinforcements from Delhi, and then to proceed towards Dholepore.

I have the honor to be,

Sir,

Your most obedient servant,

FRED. ROBERTS, Lieut.,

Offg. D.A.Q.M.General.

INDEX

THE END